Domain Sellers Handbook.
Written by Renata Barnes

D1823488

An informative guide on how to start a Domain Selling Business. It lets you know what to do and what not to do.

Every business needs a website, a domain name and marketing. Most business's want more customers and you will be able to educate your buyers to buy exact match searchable keyword domain name using my methodology.

Regardless what niche you choose to market, everyone needs a little help to get more business, hence you will find some valuable hints and tips that can help you and your prospective client succeed.

Do not take Domain Names for granted, as once they are gone they are gone forever unless you want to start Domain Acquisitions.

This book is Focused not only at Domain Sellers and Investors it is also an educational tool for Business's & Millennials.

All Companies no matter how big or small want more business and are always exploring ways to generate more Traffic.

Millennials our future entrepreneurs will find it more and more difficult to acquire their ideal domain names.

Buy buying an exact match searchable keyword you are securing your place above your competitors.

Adding the keyword domains to your seo link wheel or forwarding them to your website will generate organic traffic whilst saving you money on paid per click advertising.

TABLE OF CONTENTS

'THE DOMAIN SELLERS HANDBOOK'
Written by
'Renata Barnes'.

Disclaimer

This book has been written to provide information about self improvement. Every effort has been made to make this book as complete and accurate as possible.

Therefore, this book should be used as a guide.

The purpose of this book is to educate.

10% of the Profits of this Book Will Go to the 'Multiple Sclerosis' Charity in the UK

FIRST EDITION PUBLISHED OCTOBER 2018

Website's/Blogs:

www.startbrand.co.uk
www.ukwebsitedesigners.co.uk / www.cymrumarketing.com /
www.ukdomainbrokers.com / www.cymrumarketing.co.uk

CHAPTER ONE

About The Author.

My name is 'Renata Maziak-Barnes'., but I prefer to be known as 'Renata Barnes' as 'Maziak' is hard to spell let alone remember and is more a family name. I have had over 25 years experience in the Marketing & Media Industry. I have had my work printed in several publications and currently exhibit my work online.

I started out doing Photography and back in the day I specialized in Photojournalism, Commercial, Industrial, Editorial Photography.

My first website's I ever built were in 1993 for a security company and a photographic studio and even back then my domain names contained keyword's in them 'Siren Security' & 'Siren Photography'. They no longer exist and there was not much information back then about marketing online or seo, so I never thought that this could have been a commodity that I could have just kept and possibly sold on.

Registrars were at the time charging stupid prices to renew domain names. I remember being charged just over £250 which was just over $300 for the renewal of my domain name www.renatamaziak.co.uk year in and year out, which although I am priceless :-) my domain name unfortunately was not..........., so I eventually dropped it :-)

I decided it was time to spread my wings and was on a different journey one which would lead me to feeling content that I have finally achieved one of my goals in life and had started a business from scratch without any help from anyone else. I had finally done it on my own.

I still have a bucket list of things to do and one of them was to write this book.

I have spent many long hours reading and learning, drinking many energy drinks to keep me awake, hoarding loads of information. I am a walking encyclopedia :-) when it comes to domain names, marketing, website design and photography.

Although I hadn't abandoned photography completely, I was being asked to create website's locally for business's more and more often. So my work is a diversity of Website Design, Marketing, SEO, Domain Brokering, Graphic Design and Photography. However the knowledge I have gained as a photographer has been extremely valuable when it comes to photo editing branding and has benefited my business by enabling me to design logos and templates for the domains I broker and websites I design as well as business advertising.

I have found that if you can master many trades, you can save yourself money. Why pay for someone else to do it if you can manage to overcome your obstacles and do it yourself? From all the domains I have sold, website's I have built and logos I have designed I have saved myself a small fortune in paying staff and outsourcing work.

I was born in Shrewsbury Shropshire United Kingdom. I now live with my daughter in Cardiff.

Sadly my daughter has been diagnosed with 'Multiple Sclerosis' only a few months ago which was a devastating blow to the both of us, hence I have decided to donate 10% of the profits of this book to the 'Multiple Sclerosis' Charity.

I was born to Polish Ancestors. My father was a soldier and fought in the Second World War in 'Monte Cassino' and then with the British Army, where 'Winston Churchill' later gave him permanent residency in the UK for him and his mother to live. My mother came over just after the war had ended where my parents met whilst my mother was on holiday.

I did have two brother but sadly one passed away a few years ago and my other brother lives in Seattle in the USA.

My story is far from being a straight forward one. Lets just say what does not kill you makes you stronger and that's another book waiting to be told.

I have had a lot of devastating things happen in my life which have made me a very driven and determined. Where I had obstacles put before me I chose to get round them rather than do nothing. My work is my passion and this is what drives me to reach my goals. I have a dream board that I look at each day and I know one day I will complete everything I am reaching for.

The reason I have decided to write this book is to emphasis the importance of buying exact match searchable keyword domain names that can pro-actively help a business generate organic traffic. I also want to mention if your are making a profit you are theoretically running a business and as such you have to declare yourself self-employed and declare your earnings.

Don't get me wrong people do write about about domaining but not much about running a domain name business. Even I bought some clangers when I first started out due to miscalculations and stupidity, which I later dropped. I am not perfect by any means but I learn quickly.

You need to be first and foremost a business person, an internet marketer and know about SEO to understand the value of Domain Names. You cannot just pull figures out of a hat. Of course there are investors which will only pay minimum prices for your domains and business's do not always scour marketplaces to find their ideal keyword domain name. So you need to be aware that marketplaces will not always fetch your desired price. Hence you need to be able to do outbound marketing and that does not mean sending unsolicited emails which usually find themselves in the spam or junk folders anyway.

Also consider how many people before you have also tried contacting the same CEO's. You have to stand out and be professional.

There is more to it than simply buying and selling domain names you also have to be self employed as soon as you start making money. There are implications if you do not declare your earnings and eventually this will catch up with you.

You also have to be aware of the money laundering and terrorism act. You have to have your own terms and conditions and have legal documents in place. Our team of solicitors offer this service.

If a broker or a marketplace cannot sell your domains you have to decide if they are worth keeping or not?. You can persevere by outbound marketing yourself but you need to abide by the code of practice. CEO's are very busy therefore you need to devise a plan to reach out to them in a professional manner.

CHAPTER TWO

Introduction.

This book is the foundations of starting an online business and is also a guide to helping you stop making costly mistakes.

Consider all the factors before venturing into Buying & Selling Domain Names. Learn about SEO, SMO & Marketing before approaching businesses. You must create a good impression as first impressions are what can make you or break you.

By going into the Domain buying and selling business your are theoretically starting a business of your own of which you need to know everything about running a company. There are serious implications if you do not declare your earning and sales over £85,000 you have to be VAT Registered which is different to VAT Moss which I will come to later relating to digital products.

The Domain Brokering industry has only in recent years due to a lot of publicity become a massive money making industry. But the only people that really benefit from this are the registrars and the well informed investors.

So how do you start buying up domain names? I will give you examples and what you have to do to buy them.

Anyone and everyone seems to thinks that buying a domain name is going to make you rich, that is not the case at all. If you have an inferior name regardless of the domain extension if it won't help a business save money in PPC and drive traffic to their website you are basically flogging a dead horse.

You need some knowledge of Marketing and SEO to understand the full potential of a domain name and its purpose.

Just because people made a lot of money when the internet started to evolve does not mean it is going to happen now.

Some prices are over inflated because people are making up figures as they go along and some of the sale stats are dubious as there is no proof that the domains sold for xyz, it's just published on a website, which anyone with a bit of knowledge of website design can do. I could publish I sold a domain xyz for £££££££ amount of money, but in reality sold it for a couple of hundred pounds. I would obviously gain a lot of followers and gain a lot of traffic and publicity, but without these detailed stats of who bought what, I do not believe some of the sales, other than on marketplaces that publicly announce their sales reports, then that is obviously different. Besides a lot of domains may get sold for high figures but are bound by non disclosure agreements so my advise is do not believe everything you read online.

Occasionally you will hear of a high ticket sales but it is not very often. One word dot com's have mainly gone and the only way to extend this is to try and buy one word domain names with the extensions .net .info .org .biz However new GTLD extensions are being registered which can also benefit search engine optimization. If you can get a one word GTLD with an extension applicable to your niche or location that *flows* when you search for the keyword then you are slightly closer of being on to a winner. Your keyword or business will not be inferior to a dot com because of your GEO location. **Dot coms are for US or Global Trade Only.**

If you want to target, local or national traffic, dot coms are not for you unless you live in America that is or want to trade internationally.

What I mean by the term (flow) is that your keyword and extension are words that are part of a sentence and are search terms.

There are over 270 million domains registered to date and counting, only a fraction are premium domains. Domains are premium asset digital real estate. They give authority status and credibility. People searching for keywords will more likely choose a domain that is descriptive and will proceed it to be trustworthy.

Keyword domains have the advantage of ease to recall short name brands with less confusion.

It is not uncommon for premium domains to have sold for 6 & 7 figures, but that does not mean that your domain names will sell for high figures.

Domain names are like real estate, rather than having bricks and mortar you have a virtual property that is classed as a digital equity.

Depending on how many words are used and what extensions determines the price of your domain. The most sort after domains are the ones with one or two words or or 2 & 3 letters or numbers.

Most popular and valued tld (Top Level Domain) domain extentions are .com, .net, .org, followed by the increasingly popular .in and .cc. Try to stick with words from the english dictionary although other countries domains and language are just as crucial to their own location.

Stick to short generic words.

I recommend people to first educate themselves before venturing into the unknown. Everyone wants to sell their domains for big bucks, but unless you know what your doing and have the right connections you will be just wasting your money with renewal fees.

If your unsure if your domain will sell don't buy them until you have done your research, don't just presume they will sell when they might not and don't assume if you can't sell them that a broker will.

Brokers are not miracle workers, if your domain won't help business's save money in PPC advertising don't expect your domains to sell at all.

The name of the game is to help business's generate traffic and if your domain can't do that, then I suggest you re-evaluate your portfolio.

Domain names are like valuable coins they are collector pieces that will become more valuable over time if they been fully developed into websites generating traffic and income. The only way domains could be of value in future if words are not readily available but sought after. So if you have a one word dot com then obviously are going to be valuable but if the word is popular and all the domain extensions for that particular keyword have been bought up, this means if you hold on to your domain name eventually someone will buy it because of supply and demand for that word.

If you haven't sold your domain that your are active;y selling within 12-24 months you will have to re-evaluate your options and either take a gamble to renew your domains for however long it will take to sell them or drop them and move on to something else. Consider developing them to generate traffic whilst at the same time monetizing the website, landing page or blog. Blogs rank faster than static sites because of the frequency of new information uploaded.

It is relatively pretty easy to find investors on marketing channels like Flippa Sedo, Afternic and Godaddy to name a few. These investors do this for a living and scour marketplaces for domains to flip. So if you have not been approached it may be one of two things either your domain is worthless or the asking price is too high.

However one has to understand their are **two types of investors.**

1) The first being an entrepreneur buying a digital asset at the lowest price possible, purely to make a gain on his/her investment by selling it for a higher price.

2) The second type of investor is a company looking to either add a domain to their SEO link wheel to help them generate more business or they maybe rebranding themselves, this includes startup's which have already thought of their company name and are looking for a domain to match their business.

One also has to appreciate that a company in the UK for instance is not going to go for a dot com domain name, unless they are planning to trade worldwide. The same goes for companies in Australia are more inclined to buy a domain extension dot au rather than a dot com.

Why have traffic primarily form the USA with a dot com, when you can have targeted traffic for your location?

More often than not a UK company will look for domain extensions like .co.uk .uk .org.uk .london .wales .scotland .ie.

The same goes for domain hacks, they may look catchy and can be added as an accessory to a default branded domain name but they do not serve a purpose of generating targeted traffic to a website which is potentially what a business tries to achieve.

Examples of domain hacks are like www.exampl.es www.simp.ly Why do I say this....because search engines use complex algorithms to drive traffic by the domain extension used and this won't get you on the First Page of any search engine unless you live in Libya that is or Spain as an example with the extensions .ly and .es to name a few.

You will get traffic from the country you registered the domain extension location.

Imagine you are paying for pay per click advertising and you are located in the United States. You want targeted traffic localized in the United States for your website and you buy a hack which looks cool and potentially easy to remember and you use it in your advertising campaign. What will happen is that if say you bought a hack with the domain extension .ly you will end up with traffic from Libya and this will use up your budget as people from Libya will be clicking on your advert.

Do you see what I am saying?

Therefore I do not recommend domain hacks unless you just use them as an accessory and perhaps have them on your business card, but I would never try to brand them especially if they are associated with a different country other than your own.

My best advise is do your research. Don't give up your day job in the hope you will make millions overnight, it takes time and patience.

Once you have sold a few domains then consider your life changing goals and not before.

Once you feel confident you have a prized gem, contact organizations that may be interested in buying your domain, don't be shy and follow your gut feelings.

There are plenty of domain selling, books, e-book, blogs and advice websites out there its up to you to do your homework.

If you think you have a domain that has little value, then you most probably have got just that.

Don't bother renewing it year after year, if after you have put it up for auction you have little or no views at all, that's telling you to reconsider your options especially if you have used upgrades.

Create a landing page for each domain you have and do your SEO which is very important or have it parked page with a registrar. Consider the difference between a landing page that is search engine optimized and a parking page which is not.

Contact businesses that may be interested. *Never give up.*

Don't get me wrong buying and selling domain names can be a very lucrative business if you know what you are doing.

However if you are starting off on a small budget, it's always best to purchase lower cost domains, do remember your renewal fees before purchasing a large portfolio.

All you virtually need is to find a memorable keyword domain name which are appealing domain names in niche markets and sell them to buyers, eager to increase traffic to either invest and flip or companies or individuals that need to develop their own website for the said keywords.

Choosing Prized Domains

Choosing Domain names depends on many factors. Start-ups will look to see if their product or brand is available, companies wishing to generate more business may look for compatible keywords to link to their default site, whilst others may simply be re-branding themselves. The easiest way is to check if your domain is available to buy is to check with the the registrars or type it in the search bar. If it isn't you either choose a name with a relevant extension or in some cases even start an acquisition to try and buy the name from an existing owner. Obviously the the blue chip already branded trademarked companies are out of bounds but some smaller companies providing the price is right may sell their domain name and rebrand themselves especially if they can see a benefit in selling their domains for financial gain.

Investors looking for investments to sell for the future may scour directories of expired domain names which may be aged domains as they will be seen as trustworthy by search engines. There are many software tools available online that make the process less tedious. Here are a couple you can try:

www.justdropped.com
www.DomainPunch.com/products/domainfilter
www.Moniker.com
Also consider Godaddy Bargain Basement.

Remember that investors quickly snatch up good domains so you need to be quick and on the ball. You also need to be aware that registrars who have domain brokers working for them also analyse data and are also watching and waiting for prized domain names to be available. This is called **domain snatching** However if you see a domain name available do not think it will be around for long so if you happen to see it do not hesitate and register it straight away.

Sometimes expired domain names are not released to the public for about 7 days after expiration date, hence using an independent tool like:

www.DomainTools.com makes more sense.

When registering your domain names, make sure they are pronounceable not misspelt and easy to remember. Do not register a domain that is similar to a trademark, as it can confuse people and may be seen as misrepresentation. Also consider the following factors as some domain names have been dropped by a previous owner for a reason , one being they may have been banned by Google.

Domain Tasting and Kiting

From a marketing perspective I cannot get my head round this, so you buy a domain name you test it out for a few days and if your not happy ask for a refund, kiting is repeating the process.

I do not see the benefit of this at all, as you do your market research before you buy the domain and you will not only get a bad reputation you will also be banned by Search Engines if you make a habit of it.

You can do your due diligence by checking to see if domains you purchase have been banned by Google using the following tools:

www.SelfSEO.com
www.IWebTool.com

If you plan to make and example website / landing page and simply have it floating in cyperspace then that is fine as long as you do not upload it to any search engines and do any SEO or marketing. Sometimes we may just need to make a site as reference or an example of what a business may look like if it was fully developed.

But for Domain Names that you want to advertise, creating a landing 'For Sale' page with marketing and seo can be very beneficial to you and your future buyer. Not only will you be selling a domain name but also traffic for the related keywords.

CHAPTER THREE

Registrars.

Registrars are more than happy to have you list your domains for sale and even more happier when you actually buy a domain from them. Its big business to them and they don't care if your domain sells or not, they just want you to buy from them.... period.

They are not their to hold your hand.

If you mess up its your fault. I once bought a domain which was readily available to buy with one of the top registrars so I went ahead and bought it not thinking about the implications as at the time I did not think I was going to have any issues. I just thought it was an investment. I did not develop it, nor did I market it, I just left it in my portfolio without a landing page and did not even have it marked for sale, until one day I received an email from a company claiming that the domain I bought had in fact been cybersquatted by me. Infuriated at the suggestion they had made I went about making enquiries. I even suggested to them that the domain I had bought was a Surname and Surnames cannot be trademarked even though they were a famous brand, yet they had not trademarked themselves in Wales, how wrong was I and good job I released it when I did.

Not knowing the full extent of my actions other than that I had to release it back to this third party otherwise I would be looking at a liable suit against my company by what they claimed was from the rightful owner, I was forced into a corner to surrender the domain.

Since then I have had people contact me with similar domains and I just advise them to drop them as soon as possible.

I had to ask myself the question as it was a high brand designer company and also a surname, but they had not trademarked themselves in Wales hence I had two choices continue to keep it or surrender. I chose to surrender. I did not want to spend costly legal fees defending myself so I gave it up. I then went back to the registrar and asked why are they selling these domains if in fact they are reserved for the trademarked famous brand companies. They could not answer me other than say I should have done my due diligence. Also if these high brands are aware that these domains are for sale why do they not buy them up or have them transferred automatically to them? basically I think its a *entrapment*. These companies have their own marketing agents who are aware that these domains exist and lie in wait for their next victim. Why pay £10 or $10 for a domain if you can sue the next person that comes along for hundreds of thousands, see what I mean. Its a lame way of making money and underhanded.

Under federal trademark law, it is not possible to get a federal trademark registration from the USPTO on a mark that would be considered primarily merely a surname, or last name, unless you can establish secondary meaning (also referred to as "acquired distinctiveness").

In layman terms, this means that you would have **to establish that consumers in the marketplace now view your mark as a reference to your company, and not as a reference to your last name.** It is possible to trademark a last name, only if you can satisfactorily prove "acquired distinctiveness" to the United States Patent and Trademark Office (USPTO), otherwise you will be denied the full protection of federal law for your trademark.

How does the USPTO determine whether your mark is primarily merely a surname?

They look to several factors, including whether anyone connected to the trademark applicant has that surname, whether the mark is a **common surname**, whether the mark has any alternative definitions beyond the surname, and whether the mark has the "look and feel" of a surname when deciding if you can trademark a last name. There are multiple examples of surnames successfully going through the trademarking process; Dell, Ford, and Chanel to name just a few.

I should note that the whole purpose behind prohibiting marks that are merely surnames is to keep them available for potential applicants who want to use their own surnames as part of their business identity. As always, you should consult a competent trademark attorney/solicitor before proceeding with a trademark registration. *I recommend staying well away from Christian and Surnames Combinations as well as Surnames.*

Examples of Trademarked Surnames

To illustrate what it means to establish "acquired distinctiveness", let's look at a few examples of last names that successfully became trademarks.

Kellogg's
"Kellogg's was founded as the Battle Creek Toasted Corn Flake Company on February 19, 1906, by Will Keith Kellogg as an outgrowth of his work with his brother John

Harvey Kellogg at the Battle Creek Sanitarium following practices based on the Seventh-day Adventist Church. The company produced and marketed the hugely successful Kellogg's Toasted Corn Flakes and was renamed the Kellogg Company in 1922." (Source)

The Kellogg's name originally began as a last name, but through the popularity of its breakfast cereal it acquired a secondary meaning as a reference to the company for most people. The mark was originally filed for registration on December 15th, 1914 and was officially registered on October 18th, 1921.

McDonald's

The McDonald's story was recently dramatized in the 2016 movie, The Founder. It shows the journey of McDonald's from the single location hamburger stand run by Richard and Maurice McDonald, to what would become a worldwide brand under Ray Kroc. Through its popularity and global recognition, it isn't hard to see why the McDonald name had achieved the required distinctiveness needed to be a registered mark.

The name was originally filed for protection on May 4th, 1961. It was officially registered on January 8th, 1963 as a service mark, in the goods & services category of drive-in restaurant services.

In recent years, McDonald's has been accused of being a bit of a bully due to the aggressive and thorough manner in which they defend their various marks. Though, given the size and reach of the company, it's understandable that they would worry about consumer confusion and copying.

A more modern take on surnames addition to the list is the **Kardashian** family has used their surname in a variety of marks, covering goods and services ranging from lip gloss to retail stores. The name first appeared in a registered mark when Kim Kardashian filed to register her name in February of 2007 in the categories of both cosmetics and jewelry. The mark registered in both categories by September of the same year.

As the family's popularity continued to grow, so did their list of marks. The surname Kardashian was filed for protection on February 26, 2013 and officially registered on January 21, 2014 covering "Advertising services, namely, promoting the brands, goods and services of others; endorsement services, namely, promoting the goods and services of others."

The more general marks of the Kardashian name are typically registered by three California corporations representing each of the three oldest sisters, Kim, Khloe, and Kourtney. The company names are Kimsaprincess Inc., Khlomoney Inc., and 2Die4Kourt, respectively.

Close call and lesson learnt for me. Now I have a legal firm as part of my business for clients that may need their help. Although I do consult my clients and advise them to stay clear of famous names, brands etc. My services even offer trademark registration and company formation.

I know tell my clients if you have a famous name or company or brand stay away do not waste your money. If you have any legal issues please contact us and we will put you in touch with the law firm.

CHAPTER FOUR

What are TLD's and GTLD's

What are TLD's

A top-level domain is one of the domains at the highest level in the hierarchical Domain Name System of the Internet. The top-level domain names are installed in the root zone of the name space.

What are GTLD's

Generic Top Level domain names (*gTLDs*) are domain extensions that are alternatives to the traditional .com, .co.uk and .de domain extensions. Businesses have applied to ICANN (the organisation which oversees domain names) to operate these *gTLDs*.

The dot com industry is dominated by the USA, thats why business in the USA prefer to have dot coms unlike the UK which prefer .co.uk, .uk .wales .scotland as it would make no sense to their location unless they were planning to trade overseas.

If someone in the UK wanted to build a website they would not go for a a dot com extention, unlike someone in France or China or Russia, who may want a global audience may consider a dot com aswell as their own GEO location extension. Besides people in Russia speak Russian and will search for Russian websites and their extensions in their own language and keywords rather than an English written website. Furthermore they may use translators to change the language of the site to the visitors preference.

So there is money to be made from location domains in their own language, it would make no sense to use a word like www.knee.fr as it most probably would not be understood much less searched for unless it was marketed and branded extensively for the French market.

I learn fast and yes you can work with the big boys dominating the planet with their dot coms but country and language domains still have possibilities.

Never be afraid to take a challenge.

I was just doing my daily research and came across an interesting thread about cybersquatting and how the ordinary person whom does not understand the value of domain names accuses domain investors /brokers as cyber-squatters and how it is immorally incorrect to buy a domain at a low price and then sell it for hundreds or thousands or in some cases millions. **Granted the domain name may have been bought for a low price but time was spent finding it and then securing it as well as valuing it. So the £10 or $10 spent registering it has now has increased in price on the time spent analysing and reporting the commodity.**

In fact one of the replies refers to what I talked about earlier that location domains are an interesting way to snap up really cool keywords. Just like the guy said you need to think outside the box.....

Here is the link to the thread:
http://www.ukbusinessforums.co.uk/threads/cybersquatters-or-domain-investors.315789/

GTLDS

Extensions like .london, .cymru.. scotland, .wales, .consulting etc are getting increasingly popular.

More than 1,200 new extensions will be released over the next few years giving dot com competition, according to icann.org.

To view the latest delegated strings keep an eye on the following link which is updated as soon as the GTLD's become available. This will become useful when you want to be a step ahead:

https://newgtlds.icann.org/en/program-status/delegated-strings

Another site which is useful for inspiration is:

http://blog.europeandomaincentre.com/best-new-tld/#

Its shows how companies have tried to be unique and steered away from the traditional dot coms.

Here's a tip of my own get yourself an address book and one day take time out to search for words and extensions and when you find they are available in combinations of .com, .org, net etc write them down. Then when you have the money to invest go back to them and buy them up if they are still available.

Also keep a calendar/planner of your renewal dates, it's easy to overlook payments, although the registrars normally send out reminder notices via email well in advance to the expiration dates.

CHAPTER FIVE

What you need to know before you buy

I will first give you an example of something, I have two domainers both selling the same niche domains both are selling the domains at the same price as one another. However Domainer (a) is only selling the domain whilst Domainer (b) is selling a domain, a website and a license. Domainer (a) will not get the same money for the same niche product because he has over valued his domain name.

The moral of this is from a marketing perspective one needs to convince an investor whom may already have a website, why they should buy another domain. The most sellable ones are short, pronounceable keyword domains that actively generate traffic to a website. Domains that have acronyms are usually more difficult to sell. Imagine you are an entrepreneur you have got your idea of your business model. You have already thought up the name for your brand, you are not going to go skimming through directories of brands to buy unless you are already established and want add ons.

No startup is going to look for a brand name as 9 times out of ten they would have already invented themselves.

Their problem is to see if word or words are available to buy through the registrars. If they happen to trademark themselves and come across a brokerage firm selling their name this could lead to complications.

On the other hand Domain Investors primarily look to acquire cheap domains they can flip and majority hangout on Flippa, Godaddy, Sedo and Afternic to name a few. Free credits to these companies as I use them myself for my own personal domains.

The best way to market your domain is to have a landing page where you can do SEO and get it on the first page of Search Engines. This is a service my company can provide for a cost of £49.99 per domain per annum.

Having a parking page with Godaddy, Afternic & Sedo is all very well if a person types in you domain name directly in the search engines address bar, then granted your domain will be found or if an investor searches on marketplaces. Other than that the only benefit of having a parking page on these sites is to help the above companies rank higher as they are providng you a subdomain of their own website forwarding your domain name to them with any SEO.

It stands to reason anyone typing in the domain name into the search bar will land on the page so the only benefit to you is if someone actively types your domain to see if it is available. But what if you could drive traffic to your page this would be more proactive as you could add other keywords in the your headers and titles to get a broader scope of people potentially finding your domain name.

The best thing I can suggest is if you can build a one page website yourself and do your own SEO then good for you, but if you need some help then contact a website designer/seo expert.

Granted you may get revenue from their landing pages that the domain registars offer through the affiliate links but you share the commission between you and the registrar or brokerage firm. You may have little control what is advertised besides your domain name.

That is why it is always better to build it yourself or go to an expert.

But what if you were just putting in your keywords into Google none of these companies will go as far as doing any SEO for you and you will not be found on keywords alone only by the exact url address in the address bar. What if your were selling www.voicescanners.com but the person just typed in 'voice scanners' into the search engine, what are the chances of you being found? This domain I am brokering by the way.

Without an independent one page search engine optimized landing page / website not related to a brokerage firm or registrar the chances of your domain ever to be found are very slim unless directly searched for with the full URL address in the browsers address bar.

CHAPTER SIX

Marketing

When you buy your domain name think how it will be relevant to the end user. Do not use more than three words maximum. The fewer keywords the better, I personally prefer maximum two words, three must be an exception.

Also some domain extensions are not marketable, I will give an example what business would want to be known as www.ukdomainbrokers.wtf ? (:-) Smiley face). If I could not have www.ukdomainbrokers.com - yes before you say anything there is a domain extension .wtf - I would most certainly not use the extension as it would not perceive my company to be professional.

Also over pricing your domain names is another factor why your domains won't sell. I do not use online bots to value domain names I use the method of trusted Google Keyword Planner. You must have a gmail account to access this alternatively there is a company called www.serps.com and they give you a 30 day trial.

There I type in my keyword and domain name and Google submits how many times per month your keyword is searched for and how much it would cost per click if you paid for advertising.

Branding.
Put yourself in an entrepreneurs shoes for a minute, you have decided what business you are about to startup. You have a business plan and now you need to brand your company.

You have run out of ideas after asking your friends and family although in most case a business man/women already knows in their mind what they are going to be called.

However in the worst case scenario they turn to the web for ideas and go to branding companies for inspiration. This is like looking for a needle in a haystack, unless you are an entrepreneur that specifically scours endless lists for names that could be brandable and turned into a business which is something Web Designers and Marketers may do for affiliate marketing purposes or to set up micro sites to then sell on.

In most cases people usually turn to registrars to filter through domains that can be branded. However a scrambled made up word which has little or no meaning or acronym which is an abreviation is less likely to be ranked in search engines, unless the brand is extensively marketed that it frequently comes up in search results.

An Acronym

An acronym is a word or name formed as an abbreviation from the initial components in a phrase or a word, usually
individual letters and sometimes syllables. There are no
universal standards for the multiple names for such abbreviations or for their orthographic styling.

Examples of famous acronyms
Pronounced as a word, containing only initial letters

NATO: **N**orth **A**tlantic **T**reaty **O**rganization

Scuba: **s**elf-**c**ontained **u**nderwater **b**reathing **a**pparatus

Laser: **l**ight **a**mplification by **st**imulated **e**mission of **r**adiation

GIF: **G**raphics **I**nterchange **F**ormat

Pronounced as a word, containing a mixture of initial and non-initial letters
Amphetamine: **a**lpha-**m**ethyl**phen**ethyl**amine**
Gestapo: *Geheime Staatspolizei* ('secret state police')

Radar: **ra**dio **de**tection **a**nd **r**anging

Pronounced as a string of letters, containing syllable-initial but not necessarily word-initial letters

PMN: **p**oly**m**orpho**n**uclear leukocytes

OCA: **o**culo **c**utaneous **a**lbinism
PCM: **p**ara **c**occidioido **m**ycosis
Pronounced as a word or as a string of letters, depending on speaker or context

FAQ: (frequently asked questions
IRA: When used for Individual Retirement Account, can be pronounced as letters (*i-ar-a*) or as a word [ˈaɪrə].
SQL: ([siːkwəl] or *ess-cue-el*) Structured Query Language.
Pronounced as a combination of spelling out and a word

CD-ROM: (*cee-dee*-[rɒm]) Compact Disc read-only memory

IUPAC: (*i-u*-[pæk] or *i-u-pee-a-cee*) International Union of Pure and Applied Chemistry

JPEG: (*jay*-[pɛg] or *jay-pee-e-gee*) Joint Photographic Experts Group

SFMOMA: (*ess-ef*-[moʊmə] or *ess-ef-em-o-em-a*) San Francisco Museum of Modern Art

Pronounced only as a string of letters:

BBC: British Broadcasting Corporation
OEM: original equipment manufacturer

USA: United States of America

A Made Up Name

(Examples of Famous Brands that had their names made up)

Have you ever wondered what is the meaning behind the famous brands that we see today and how they were made up and by whom?

Adidas
Is a nickname of founder Adolf 'Adi' Dassler

Adobe Systems

Named after Adobe Creek, a stream which ran behind the house of one of the co-founders, John Warnock.

Amazon
Amazon was named after the most voluminous river in the world. Giving a description of enormousy.

Amstrad
Alan **M**ichael **S**ugar**Trad**ing

Accenture
Accenture resulted in a competition amongst staff to come up with a name tp describe 'Accent on the future'.

Aldi
The surname of the founders (**Al**brecht) plus **di**scount

Coca-Cola
The name and drink was derived because of the *cocaine* leaf and kola fruits that *were* used to add flavour. Dr. Pemberton's partner and bookkeeper, Frank Robinson, suggested the *name* "*Coca-Cola*" because he thought using the letter C twice would look better than if they used a K in the *word* "*Cola*".

Danone
Danone is the founders first son **Dan**iel + **one**

Datsun
Originally DAT, changed to Datson implying a smaller version of the car, then changed to Datsun (as son can mean 'loss' in Japanese) when acquired by Nissan

Equifax
Equitable and factual

Garmin
After its founders **Gar**y Burrell and Dr. **Min** Kao

Haagen-Dazs
Haagen-Dazs the popular Ice-cream company made-up 'European sounding' name designed to 'convey an aura of old-world traditions and craftsmanship'

Intel
Meaning **Int**egrated **El**ectronics

Lego
A play on the Danish expression, *Leg godt*, which means, *Play well.*

Lycos
From *Lycosidae*, the family of wolf spiders

Nike
Nike the popular sport brand takes its name from Nike, the Greek goddess of victory

Pixar
From pixel and the co-founder's name, Alvy Ray Smith

Samsonite
Samsonite luggage which is renowned for its robust quality was named after the Biblical character Samson, renowned for his strength.

Starbucks
Named after Starbuck, a coffee loving character in Herman Melville's novel Moby Dick

Twitter
Twitter was a combination words of early name such as, Twitch and Jitter which evoked the impression of receiving

a tweet over SMS

Vodafone

From Voice, Data, Telephone

Branded Domain Names
For a domainer as I pointed out to one of my clients today after he asked for my advice if he should drop one of his domains, I recommended that he should as it had little meaning. Therefore unless you know for a fact that your made up word will sell I would avoid buying such domains.

Also a word of advice do not use famous people's names or brands in your domain names ie for example: nikeshoes or netflixmovies as it has a trademark in the keyword or

could be similar and misleading to an original brand. I have had many discussions about this and registrars sell trademark domains and extensions even though they know that anyone buying them may be liable to be sued. They do not care as it is up to you to take that risk and it's money to them if you buy that name, it called business even though I think it's unethical.

Contraban - Illegal Substances & Firearms Domain Names.
Marajuana or any other type of illegal drugs comes to mind - if you intend to buy such a domain and then sell it on your own directly to an investor consider the implications if it is a buyer from a country which has not legalized the drug i.e UK wants to buy it, you have to do your due diligence and ask what the investor wishes to use it for.

Unless the buyer intends to flip the domain for an investment to another investor of a legalized state or country it is unadvisable to promote the drug even if it is only the domain name that you are selling, as the buyer may use it as an e-commerce tool.

This may be deemed as incitement to commit a crime and aiding and abetting. If you sell it through one of the leading auction sites most likely it will be an investor that will buy the domain to flip for a profit and not the pimp in your local hood.

This is a very grey area which no one seems to talks about. Be cautious and always put a disclaimer saying that you will not be liable for prosecution if it ends up in the wrong hands and the digital trail links back to you. ICANN keeps your details on their servers which are shared with the people that need to know. The same goes for 'Streaming Domains' most streaming domains are illegal - do you want the Police knocking your door 5am in the morning? - *stay away from domains that can be interpreted as something illegal.

Guns which are obviously illegal in the UK and also should be in the USA in my opinion especially after the shootings in Florida and are also are a topic of discussion worldwide. If you have a domain with a 'Gun' related keyword ask yourself who are you going to sell it to?, if it is a domain investor that intends to flip it b2b then providing you have proof of this, then this is ok, however if it is 'Joe Blogs' off the street in a country where guns are illegal you have to be cautious as you could be inciting someone to commit a crime.

Always do your due diligence, and put a liability disclaimer of professional indemnity more commonly known as errors & omissions (E&O) in the US stating you will not be liable for third party misuse of the domain name.

Always protect yourself!

CHAPTER SEVEN

Social Media

Social Media Traffic Generation Tips

The Internet is a social place. Although everything is done in the virtual world, the place is swarming with social networks, social media sites and social opportunities to target your niche market and network with the right prospects. So why not take advantage of the social nature of the net by using social media as a way to generate traffic and target your niche. Below I have listed some of the top tips in the subject of social media traffic.

1) Stand out from the crowd: get noticed by developing your new site, add exciting new content on social bookmarking sites. Many social bookmarking sites, such as Digg, Reddit etc are read on a daily basis and a perfect place to start your traffic generation debut.

2) Take advantage of free classified ads: Craig-list, Gumtree, Brown-book, Locanto etc, is a great place to get your new website noticed. Most classified ads have free listings where you can make an ad for your website, for free!

3) Get Social: start creating as many social networking accounts as possible. Social networking is a great way to get your product or service noticed. Set up a LinkedIn Page, a Facebook Page, a Yahoo Page and so on. Ask your friends to add your page as "fans" and watch your traffic grow.

Instagram is another way to show off your domains, create a business account and do screenshots of your domain names and post them, obviously a picture says a thousand words so being visual with you domain names will get you more noticed.

4) Use Stumble-upon Submit your site to Stumble Upon and then get your friends to stumble on it as well.

5) Create a Google Hangout- join or create a campaign in your area of interest. Most likely others in that group will be interested in knowing about your website and checking out what you have to offer.

6) Create a Twitter Account - Tweet your domains to your followers. Twitter combines social media with text messages with the Internet. It may seem a little over-whelming, but it's a great way to advertise your domain names quickly.

7) Join Forums – join in groups and conversations and start your own posts. This is one of the best ways to use social media in your favour. Make a brief contribution to Forums in your topic of interest. Include a link to your website after expressing your opinion or advice. However, make sure you are professional and courteous. Do not repeat yourself and don't spam.

8) Search for relevant networking sites- there are literally hundreds of networking sites for everyone and everything literally in every niche you can think of, from baby boomers to music lovers and for avid photographers, to domain marketplaces, this is where you will find your prospects.

9) Show your interest – join groups in other social media outlets, participate showing you are genuinely interested in the subject. The more comments you share, the more you will be respected and revered as an active member in your niche market community.

10) Add the social media bookmarks and share buttons on your website/landing page. This is a simple function that allows people to easily connect to your website and inform others about it. In the cyber world, word of click is just as important as word of mouth.

CHAPTER EIGHT

Blog Marketing Traffic Generation Tips

One of the best ways to get your niche audience to your landing page is to target them with blog posts.

Blogs get ranked much faster than websites due to having regular information rather than websites that may not change for many years. Search engines prefer fresh content.

There is no point developing a full blown website for each domain name you have. It is far better to create a landing page for each of your domain names to start the ball rolling
for the prospect buyer generating traffic for them, whilst attracting prospective buyers for you.

You could also consider blogs for each category or even one for your whole portfolio.

Article marketing or blog posts are a perfect way to use your words to drive traffic to your site. Essentially you (or hired content writers) can write about a topic directed at your site and include a bio and a link to your website. Article marketers will submit articles to article directories

When someone uses Google, Bing or any other search engine, often these blogs will pop up and they will click on them. What this means is that only those interested in the material in the blogs are reading the content. They will also be more interested to click through to the link (your page).

and continue to read, as long as you write and target your articles properly. Article marketing, when properly executed can generate your traffic in a matter of days!

1) Write content people will actually read, unfortunately there is a lot of rubbish on the internet so you need to be careful and investigate several sites to get a better understanding of what you are searching for. Many people attempt to use blogs or article marketing to simply write about anything and everything. Write only valuable informative content and not the first thing that's come in your mind. Be professional and be an expert. Do you research thoroughly before giving advice.

2) Use keywords. Keywords are searched for words that will get your blog noticed on search engines. Make your keywords specific and use them about 2-5% in each article, any more than this and your blog could begin to sound like an advertisement, or you could even get penalized by search engines, potentially being removed.

3) Beware of black hat listing. Marketing directories use algorithms to ensure that marketers are not simply sending them low value content. If you use too many keywords then you could be banned from the article directory and your articles not accepted. This is a complete and total waste of time so follow the rules of the directory and don't try to out smart them

4) Don't advertise, Give valuable information- the main point of your blog is to direct your prospects to your website; however, you want to do this by proving that you actually know what you are talking about and have something informative to say. No one wants to be caught in an article-advertising trap.

5) Don't spin your content, what I mean by this is copying and pasting someone else;s information and then going to www.spinbot.com and rewriting it. Although it is tempting to copy content and then spinning it, you are not in theory providing your prospects with anything new.

6) Establish yourself as an expert- give your readers an opportunity to trust you. Write a short bio about yourself, it does not have to go into too much detail but give your readers the chance to establish a connection.

7) Make sure your blogs are written well. If they are not, then can devalue your site and end up with a high bounce rate, which can damage your ranking.

8) When writing your articles express yourself with a friendly voice- make connections with your audience by speaking like them. Colloquial language is okay in certain situations; as long as you are not offending anyone, all I would avoid it if I wanted to stay professional.

8) When writing blog posts put your links at the beginning of your articles as not everyone will read the way through.

9) Gain trust from your audience write about real-life situations. make your writing relatable. Think like your audience would when writing your posts and you will have a better chance convincing them to continue to click through to your website.

10) Gain respect from your audience Make them laugh- reading something that is humorous on the web is always welcoming. This is one of the best ways to gain to convince your readers to click to your site.

11) Headers are one of the most important parts of SEO. You need to make sure your title uses the keywords you have chosen and is specific enough to be noticed by search engines.

12) Use Categories on your blog so that your audience can find what they want more efficiently. Use sub headings in chronological order. This makes sense when you have many domains in your portfolio but only one landing page.

13) Add a picture, create a logo. Logos are visual advertisements. If you can't do it yourself hire someone on fiverr.com to do it for you. You will also be saving your prospect buyer money hiring a Graphic Designer to design their brand.

14) Always check for spelling errors and proofread all your work. There is nothing worse than reading through an a website or blog that has grammatical and spelling errors. It does not look professional. Always re-read your work. This does not mean simply pressing the spell check button. It means reading it top to bottom and catching all of those hidden mistakes.

15) Remain up to date with your content, no one wants to read old news. Stay up to date on the political and current event trends.

16) Expore different writing angles - there are so many different angles you can take when writing a blog post. While some choose to write informative tips, others choose to write something controversial to really get the readers going. Consider what will benefit your audience.

17) Consider Using 'Top Ten' Article Lists - "Top" lists attract audiences to quickly skim through great articles because the reader knows exactly what they are looking for in an instance. As an example Top Ten dot co dot uk domains sold or Top Five Domain Brokers, Top 100 Most Expensive Domain ever sold.

Blogs are very useful for getting ranked quickly so consider writing about your portfolio or make individual blogs relevant for your domain name and write topics of interest. Blogs are becoming the most common type of Internet content. This is because blogging does not require the use of formal writing patterns such as newspaper articles or websites which have to be meticulous in the content they write. Blogging allows a person to enter emotion and common language and does not necessarily have to watch out for P's & Q's, without experiencing the harsh critics that the traditional article would receive. Blogs are used to provide additional content and information on a landing page from a website. Most blogs are written by professionals who specialize in the niche content. This helps to ensure that the individual is able to truly use the keywords in the appropriate percentages and still achieve a fluid conversation tone. The blogs are often grouped together and older blogs are stored on the website. This allows all of the blogs to increase the SEO ranking of the website.

The visitors to the website also find the blogs helpful as they can convey information quickly and go back for resources. This is a pivotal means of communication between the producer, seller and customer.

CHAPTER NINE

Pay Per Click (PPC) Traffic Generation Tips

Pay per click or PPC marketing is a way for both the advertiser and the website owner to benefit. To truly get the most out of PPC marketing, it's a good idea to become both the advertiser and the affiliate marketer.

What I mean is, create ad copy using PPC, but also offer PPC on your website so other relevant ads can pop up on your site. This is called affiliate marketing.

This will bring in an additional income and even residual if it is a monthly or yearly subscription to a product or service, especially if your website is generating a lot of traffic.

PPC advertisements work with pay per click meaning, as the advertiser, you only pay if someone clicks on your ad. Essentially, you are only paying for prospects and not for every single surfer who stumbles upon your ad.

This is a revolutionary way to advertise as you are literally only paying for those who actually stop by your online store.

PPC marketing works with keywords and keywords phrases. By following these tips below, you can discover how to generate traffic to both your site and your PPC ads and thus multiple your traffic and your return on investments (ROI).

1) Know the search engines- when PPC marketing, you need to deliver your PPC ads to the right places. The top five browser sites are Google, Yahoo, Bing, Microsoft Edge and Ask . Make sure you target all five of these plus many more. Most people just use Google, which is great as Google does control more than 50% of all searched material; however, what about the other 50%? There are in fact websites that offer search engine submissions for free for up to 20 search engines. If you want to submit to more then you obviously must will have to pay

2) Understand keyword bidding - keyword bids, this is crucial when it comes to valuing domain names as you need to know how much each word costs. However keywords prices change constantly change. You can either continue to check it out every day manually, or invest in bid management software, which can watch the different bids so you remain on top for each campaign you publish. Obviously the more popular the keyword is and the amount of searches it has per month will determine the final price which usually is very high,

3) Find a happy medium in bidding- when you are bidding for keywords, you need know that a some point your keyword bids may drop in price as well as searches. If you bid too high, then you are simply wasting a lot of money; however, if you bid too low then you ad may not even appear at all or if it does it will be the third page or even further down (and who goes further than the second page)? So, aim for the 5th to the 15th position. This will keep more money in your budget and ensure that you remain in a good viewing spot.

4) Stay away from Bid wars when publishing a campaign. Bid wars are usually your your competitors fighting with you to get to spot number one. However, it's best to simply step down. Bid wars do not benefit anyone except for the publisher.

5) Become a PPC expert- PPC marketing is not for everyone and not everyone understands it. Consider getting some help with PPC marketing companies. Read books, there are plenty of free e-books available, attend seminars and spend some time with a PPC consultant to help and guide you on the right direction.

6) Research the competition- I recommend www.seospyglass.com for this, there's nothing wrong with a little competitive spying. See what your competitors are doing with their websites and advertisements- what keywords are they using? What affiliate organizations are they using? Are they using Adsense? Analyse and adapt and change to suit your website and your campaigns. This is one of the smartest ways of getting ahead of the competition.

7) PPC marketing is not all directed at search engines. You also want to affiliate yourself with some of the best affiliate programs around such as 'Rakuten Linkshare' for example to ensure that your ads are being placed with the right people and places.

8) Be careful how you advertise don't bore your audience be precise and to the point and don't bombard all your products, services, and listings in one advertisement. Advertisements should be targeted towards one fast selling service or product. The advertisement on this one item will draw the prospect to the website, where you will advertise all your products or services offered. Using exact match keywords for your products and services will get you more generated traffic.

9) Create a landing page for each of your AdWords - Instead of always linking to your home page, link to various different web pages. Link to various product pages for the different AdWords you choose. For example, if you have a domain name you wish to promote which is linked to a subdomain of your website, then link your AdWords to the page that the domain is forwarded to.

10) Understand keyword buckets for Ad Group- what I mean by is that you should always create Ad groups for your different keywords. By enabling this method you can test and track the different Ad Groups and see which keyword phrase is best performing.

11) Ensure Rich Keyword Content- make sure you advertisement is rich in keywords. Its as esay as that. This is where exact match keyword domains are useful.

12) Monitor your Ads quality score, quality scores will rate all your keywords. If you have a keyword that has a 'poor' quality score, then it's a good idea to remove it as this will let your Campaign down.

13) Be unique and use DKI- this is a great little seo trick. (DKI, or dynamic keyword insertion), will insert certain words into your copy as the prospect types it in. This means that your ad copy will appear with the exact same keyword phrase type- hence your advertisement will look like it was created just for that particular person. Ad copy is a term that describes the main text of a clickable advertisement, whether it is a contextual or a pay per click ad. The text of the ad copy usually has two to three lines of an ad displayed on a search engine results page or any other web page, and is between the title and the display URL.

14) Be liberal with Keywords - many people choose just one keyword per advertisement. It's a better idea to be generous with your keywords in your ad. Two to three keywords per advertisement is more effective in reaching a wider audience and also ensures that your advertisement copy flows a little better. No one wants to be bombarded with the same keyword every second word.

15) Use all types of keywords- learn the different types of keywords that include exact match, phrase match and negative keywords. Look through Google Adwords to understand the difference between each one and determine how and where these keyword matches will help you.

16) Create a negative keyword list- negative keywords are incredibly important in advertising to ensure that the right ads pop up with the right person. By using negative keywords you are doing the opposite and informing your readers what you are "not" selling and thus targeting the right type of people.

17) Do your due diligence ask people what they look for in advertisements. Ask friends, ask family members- it never hurts to ask, and sometimes they might come up with some good ideas.

18) Geo-target- for those who have a specific area where your niche market is located, for example, in Wales, then you can geo target your advertisements to people connected from there. If your domain extension as a dot Wales but you want to target only people in Poland this will be very difficult as you will not be able to stop the traffic coming from the Wales even if your location for targeted traffic is set for Poland.

19) Google Analytics is the best tool for tracking your website traffic as well as your PPC advertisements, although Adwords do have reporting especially for your campaigns- it's important to know who and where your customers are coming from, even in the virtual world. Furthermore, tracking your ROI and your clients can help you tweak your campaign marketing strategy to gain even more prospects. You can even get precise reporting from the time of day your campaign was clicked on to what devices and operating systems where uses.

20) Always monitor your campaigns and optimize them for the best performance. Never stop tweaking PPC marketing. You need to constantly test, amend and change your campaigns in order to compete with the millions of other advertisements being put out each day.

21) Do A/B testing- PPC marketing. Optimizing and testing helps to get the best performance from your advertisements. A/B testing is one of the best ways to monitor your campaigns within Ad Groups. Create at least 2 Adcopies per Ad group and let them fight each other for the most traffic.

22) Make sure your landing page is correctly set out- this may seem simple but you need to ensure that your advertisement actually goes to the right website landing page. If you are advertising a certain product, perhaps link that that product's web page (subdomain) rather than your home page.

For example instead of linking to the homepage of 'Startbrand', link to the marketplace page. People do not have time to browse your website thoroughly they need quick and easy access. If they like what they see, then they will most likely continue to browse your website and check out the other pages, even buy.

CHAPTER TEN

Vlogging

Make a video that is educational and entertaining.

When it comes to selling Domain Names don't just think the only place you can sell on is Social Media, Forums, Marketplaces and Websites. Become an expert in your niche. So you have developed your website/landing page but you could also have a fact based video talking about Domaining and Investing. You could then have a link in the comments section directing your traffic to your portfolio or domain name. Where better to start than on YouTube and

the best thing is if you get enough views YouTube will pay you for the adverts you have linked.

1) Design & Edit your profile page

Optimize your profile page. Unlike Facebook and Twitter, you have greater freedom when it comes to customizing your YouTube profile page. Take advantage of this to make your page look more attractive to other users. You want to generate viewers that can turn into investors right, so why not make your page eye catching. You need to be creative with your page design. However, you must do so in a professional way. Do not just be clumsy and throw things in. Put some finesse into it. Your viewers will appreciate this and will think that you pay serious attention to 'quality'.

2) Hire an expert to do the task

Do you feel that this may be a little overwhelming consider hiring a professional to deign it for you? A good place to look is on www.fiverr,com or www.freelancer.com

3) Change page design according to season / event / holiday

An attractive design will not stay attractive for too long. This applies to your websites, blogs and landing pages also. When its Christmas make it Festive. People usually get tired of the same layout and search engines appreciate your creativity and frequent changes. Offer something new by changing your page design according to season/ event/holiday (e.g. Christmas theme, Halloween theme, Sales day theme, etc.).

4) Less is More.

In your pursuit to having a perfectly designed page, you might end up overdoing things. This is a mistake that many
online marketers make. The result? Their page looks unattractively shabby.

The Crowd Control Expert

5) Include a list of policies - Troll Alert.

YouTube commenters are mostly anonymous opening a massive can of worms. Although bad publicity is sometimes good publicity no one really wants people who have nothing better to do than to stalk and troll you. Therefore, you must clearly state in your T&C's page what behaviour you will not tolerate.

6) Delete damaging comments

Despite posting a list of terms and conditions, some people will be arrogant enough to ignore your request and will still do as they please. You should always be vigilant for destructive comments regardless if they targeted on you or between the people themselves. Remove all negative comments at once before anyone else sees them.

7) Hire a page manager.

Sometimes life gets in the way and you don't have time to manage your channel. Therefore, it might be an idea to hire a page moderator – someone who will maintain the page on your behalf.

8) Be polite and Courteous at all times

We sometimes have to reply to emails, letters and comments. Be professional at all times. You may need to reply to the questions of some of your viewers and subscribers. When you do, you should always be polite and courteous. Even when you have a rude or obnoxious person do not stoop to their level. Be the bigger person.

9) Ban abusive users

Abusive people do exist in the virtual world as well as in the real life. Regardless of your terms and conditions some people cannot help themselves and get a kick at hurling abuse. So if a user is repetitively abusive, you have the option of banning him/her from your page.

10) Restrict Thumbs Up if necessary

You have the option of turning off the Thumbs Up feature. This can be deemed as sarcastic or ignorant, decide if this feature is for you.

11) Use a company logo and name

Viewers are more likely to trust you if you show professionalism, show that you are not an amateur and that you know what you are talking about. A viewer prefers to see and know that the product you are reviewing or the service you are promoting is done by a professional If you slap a 2 minute video of you in the back garden people are most likely not even going to bother viewing your video especially if they do not see a company name, logo or brand. Remember to design a professional YouTube page with your company logo and name. Make sure that it also appears in each of your videos also.

12) Get rid of spammers immediately

Control how many times the same comments are made by the same people. If you are unable to control spams, people will think that you are not capable of maintaining your page. This will damage your credibility and how people view you.

13) Create a Backlink

Show authenticity and provide people a link that will direct them to your company's official website (if you have one) or blog. Also, your official website must provide a link that will direct people to your YouTube page.

14) Presentation Matters

If your videos are not professional people will not take you seriously. Low quality videos are the be all and end all of you v-logging career.

15) Make an introduction video

Introduction are important. You need to make an entrance and let your viewer know what to expect from you video's. Make at least one video that welcomes YouTube users to your YouTube page. It must be delivered by one of the top officials of your company (owner, manager, supervisor, CEO, etc.).

Searchable Content.

16) Use tags/hash tags

Keywords play an important role in all sectors of the virtual reality realm. Videos you upload will likely stay invisible in the video archives of YouTube if you do not add keyword tags describing your video. Make sure your video's are visible by adding as many tags as possible.

17) Create hashtags

What single keyword searchable terms should you use as tags? If your video talks about domain investing, use words like domain, investors, business, etc.

18) Title headers

Regardless if you are developing a website or a video on YouTube, the title of your video will also determine if your video is hard to find or not. Make sure that your video's title is rich with keyword and best describes the content of the video.

19) Adding Content

Consider adding keywords in your description box. Keywords will help target people to your video.

20) Forward related pages to your friends and subscribers.

Friends and subscribers who receive related pages to your market niche especially If those pages already have a large subscriber following will benefit you as you are exposing your page to their subscribers. Maybe some of them will subscribe to your page as well once they view the new content.

CHAPTER ELEVEN

FACEBOOK

1) Harvest 'Likes'

Once you have built your Facebook Page, invite all your friends to like your page. Once they have interacted put

something meaningful for them to share. Ask them to share your page for you. Remember to use keywords in your titles. Expose your page not only to subscribers (people who liked your page) but also to the people that are in their friends list. This is a powerful advertising tool to generate traffic. Consider running competitions or adding videos to get your audience hooked.

2) Keep subscribers entertained.

A boring page will not get your audience loyalty. Always keep them up to date with all the news and reviews with frequent posts. Your posts should also be professional if you are adverting domain names. Domain Investors are going on your page to see what you have for sale not to watch some prank video.

3) Be consistent and write content that is applicable to your niche.

Do not recycle old content or spin new ones from some one else's posts. Search engines and social media platforms use sophisticated algorithms that check for plagiarism. They can spot a spin-ned article and you do yourself no favours as they won't be that keen to promote you, even going as far as penalizing you.

4) Open a group account instead

Stay away from your personal Facebook account when promoting your domain names and create a business page. There are alternatives to a Business Facebook Page by having a Facebook Group Page where people can join and post their own content. For business related purposes, a group account offers more useful features (e.g. advertisement feature).

5) Show Credibility

Do not set up fake accounts you are potentially running a business and you want people to trust you. Be professional at all times. Anyone can make a Facebook account and put the name of your business on it. Marry up your website to your Facebook Page to show authenticity.

6) Be polite and professional

Showing the world you are trustworthy goes a long way in telling your subscribers that you mean business. Your subscribers will be confident in using you and taking your advise. Always act polite and professional and avoid childish and silly jokes in your posts and comments (unless it is part of the marketing strategy). Don't bite when you get a troll. Trolls have nothing better to do so its best to avoid conflict. Message them privately to try and resolve any issues. The way you respond to your subscribers will largely contribute to your company's public image. If you start hurling back ammunition to unhappy customers this will reflect your company image. It is important that you maintain a 'polite' mannerism in order to win the heart of your subscribers.

Also, they will admire and commend you this way.

7) Advertise successes

Consider announcing your sales stats for the domain names you have sold. You do not need to go into too much detail especially if you have non disclosure agreements with your clients but you can give an idea of how much a domain like yours can be sold for.

9) Avoid posting negative and potentially insulting comments

Taking care of your image means avoiding things that will your company a bad reputation. Therefore, it is important that you steer clear from negative comments and insulting words.

10) Avoid confrontations

Consider the feeling of your viewers. Showing unprofessionalism does nothing for your business other than getting bad publicity. Topics that touch religion, politics, and racial issues will almost always result in an argument. Avoid posting anything related to such controversial topics. If your domains result in any of the topics mentioned, be to the point and do not elaborate too much as you would be opening up a mine field for trolls to throw ammo your way. Ask yourself: 'is the post potentially offensive to someone?' If you will be advertising a skin whitening product for example, do you think for example it is wise to openly say that fair skin is better than dark skin tone? Be careful of your wording. You are in control of your own advertising company. Words can either make or break an Ad.

11) Control your targeted audience

Facebook has a setting on its advertising to choose if you want to target male or female or both. It also has a setting for age groups and locations. If you are selling women's clothing domain or have a portfolio of clothing domain names for example, you are probably just wasting money by advertising to the male audience of Facebook unless they are cross dressers. However you should also consider that you should also advertise to other groups. When it comes to women's clothing for example, you may also want to reach husbands and boyfriends who are looking for gift ideas for their partners or even sons for their mothers or grandmothers. Therefore, it is important that you are precise and scale down the scope of your advertisement to your targeted audience (Don't waste your money on unrelated categories as you pay Facebook more for this without getting a return on investment.

12) Be Creative with your Advertising

Use catchphrases and hashtags to capture your audience attention. Be original and be descriptive. Give as much information as you can to detail why people should by your domain name.

17) Connect to related groups and pages

Do not just wait for Facebook to bring your traffic to you. Reach out to your audience by joining groups and liking pages. You can then interact with other people. If you are selling women's bags domain names for example, you can like pages of businesses that sell bags, shoes etc. This way, your page will be exposed to the subscribers of those related pages. Consider sending private messages to the page owner stating the benefits of owning your domain name. Make yourself more proactive to the subscribers of related Facebook pages and groups. You can like other peoples posts or comment in a way that other people will check you out.

18) First Impressions Count

People are judgmental. People make decisions on how you look and how your business looks. If you dress untidily or have a messy office people will make decisions on first impressions. Although you should not judge a book by its cover you should make your business look smart and professional. The same goes with the content you write, if your wording is out of character, misspelt or even corny people will not take you seriously.

19) Use images and photos to spice up your posts

Be careful of copyrighted stock images. Try to be as visual as possible and make your domain names colourful and imaginative. A logo is a brand that people remember if you can make your domain name stand out people are more likely to buy it. You have potentially saved them the work of getting a designer to create one for them. A picture says a thousand words.

20) Use videos instead of plain text

When promoting your Facebook page use videos with slide shows, add some audio and create captivating adverts of all your domain names but remember to target the right audience.

21) Learn to use the 'Starred Post' feature

Your timeline is usually the first place people will go to view your profile and it is divided into the left and right side. A standard post normally takes only one side of your page. However if you 'star' a post, it will use the entire area of your page (left and right side). This way, the post will be more viewable. This is useful if you want to make your post noticeable..

22) Learn to use the 'Pinned Post' feature

Consider a 'pinned post' feature which is unlike the 'starred post', the 'pinned post only takes one side of your timeline profile. A 'pinned post' on the other hand will take the uppermost side of the page making it noticeable.

23) Utilize storage space using YouTube

Facebook do not give you much storage for your videos and images hence try using links from your YouTube channel rather than directly uploading to Facebook. This way you will save on space to upload text content and shared content. Also delete old posts especially if you have sold the domain names or dropped them, otherwise you are going to mislead your audience in to thinking the domain names are still available.

24) Consider Peoples Time

You want to engage with people but you do not want to have lengthy videos that go and on. Be precise and to the point. If you have a portfolio sideshow do not show more than 10 domain names. People as well as being busy want to view things quickly lengthy and usually do not have the patience to watch more than 20 seconds. Keep your videos professional, precise, short, detailed and to the point.

25) Be creative with your Designs

Business people are not going to look at amateur videos or video clips that are not appropriate in the theme that does not portray the niche you are trying to promote. Consider the background music, having loud heavy metal or nursery rhymes may not be suitable to business professionals such as managers, supervisors, and CEOs.

26) Use subtitles on your videos

Consider people who are hard of hearing especially if you are doing a voice over in your video. Also some people may not find it convenient to listen to your content but may want to read what you are saying. Subtitles are useful in situations where it is not possible to listen to a video especially if you are in a public place due to background noise etc.

27) Create Professional Quality Video's.

If you do not have the equipment or time or even knowledge to create a professional video, there are people on the web that can create them for you such as on www.fiverr.com Outsource your work and get them to create high quality videos on your behalf that gives your audience a lasting impression. Always authenticate your videos with your own company name and logo Your videos should start with your company credentials to show authenticity. Although high quality videos with high frame rate, high sound bitrate, and high-definition encoding are definitely the best option to give your audience, sadly, not all users can view such videos in this format so record your videos in different qualities giving the user the choice to choose which format they prefer. Do not assume everyone has access to high quality playback, as some people use computers with low specifications and internet connection that is not very fast.

28) Find the most-searched keywords in your category

To be an SMO (Social Media Optimization) expert, you must have extensive knowledge about keyword analysis and planning. You also have to be good in marketing and generating keywords. You can do this using Google AdWord – a tool that can generate the most searched keywords for a particular market. You can use the generated keywords to write SMO powered articles.

29) Include the main keyword in the your headers

Just like domain names that have one or two keywords, your titles of your articles also have to have keywords. This will benefit your Facebook page which will have better chances of making it to the top search results of Google when someone searches for a related keyword. Facebook pages are free to create they are like micro websites so take advantage and create Facebook pages for each individual domain name you own. This will save the buyer of your domain name time creating a Facebook Page and will also increase the value of your domain. If you create a website or a Facebook page your are not only generating organic traffic to your domain name you are also helping your future investor gain visitors.

30) Include the main keyword in the URL

You are potentially creating a free url courtesy of Facebook or micro website address. Marry it up with your
domain name you are selling. This has the same effect as including your main keyword in your title page. Facebook will automatically give you an URL sub domain name when you sign up. You can change this in the settings. Replace the default URL sub domain name and include the main keyword on the new sub domain.

31) Use secondary keywords in your regular posts

If for example I was using the keywords 'Export Horses' as my title tag and also in my domain name and url that Facebook had given me, if the main keywords were to be used in the URL and title page, where will you use the secondary keywords? You can use them in the short articles that you post. So for example you would use keywords such as 'Equestrian' or Thoroughbreds etc as the secondary keywords in your articles

32) Do not give up quality of your writing when

integrating keywords phrases

When writing articles do not fill your content full of keywords or use repetitive words as this lowers the quality and sincerity of your article. Quality of your article should still be your priority.

33) Keywords Analytics

I personally use Google keyword planner to manage my clients budgets for paid per click advertising and Google change the scores of the keywords on a daily basis. This means that the most searched for keywords change after some time. As such, AdWords may not generate the same results as it did a week or even a day ago. Therefore the popularity and the price of the keywords will change on a frequent basis.

34) Post RSS feeds of related news articles

Look out for up coming events and news articles from reputable sources. Consider sharing this with your viewers. This is one way to engage your viewers to be tuned to your page. If you see an online article that is related to your market niche it would be a good idea to share that page on your Facebook Page or your blog post.

35) Share related video clips

Some businesses talk about their products and services via video clips. If you find articles that are of value to your audience post links to the clips on your Social Media Pages such as Facebook etc.

36) Announce Events, Competitions and Promotions through your Facebook page

Consider offering discounts on your domain name sales. Say for the month of January for example you will give 10% off the sale of your domain names or say you offer leasing for as little as £50 per month depending on the currency of your country. Post your offers on your Facebook Page, remember try to use charm pricing instead of for instance saying £50 say £49.99 its only a penny less but it looks cheaper than the original price. Even do a competition and value a domain name with the view of winning it if your page is shared and you reach 100,000 likes for instance. Someone will then be chosen randomly and will have the domain name transferred to them free of charge with preferably one years registration.

37) Announce business changes through your Facebook page

A Facebook Page being a micro site is a convenient way to annoyance changes quickly in your business such as new domain names, days closed, service hours, etc. If you announce them through your Facebook page it will not only informs your subscribers, but it will also alleviate the authenticity of your page efficiently. Also it is easy to do using your smart phone.

38) Be Transparent

A subscriber needs to gain trust in you so do not hide your location. Allow users to see your administration office address. Be transparent enough by revealing the physical address of your office and allow users to be able to contact you via email, Skype and mobile phone.. This will also help with authenticity.

39) Reveal only the contact information of the office
Be careful of what you share. Only give out your company details and protect your administration staff with professional email addresses. If they have a dedicated email address used for the sole purpose of entertaining customers, you may disclose that email ID then.

40) GDPR

Do not share information about your staff without their prior permission keep all clients information under lock and key. Avoid identity theft, you should be discreet in withholding information about your admins, employees and investors. People with ill intention may use the personal information of other people for their benefit. The information can be used for cloning, scamming, and deceiving. Do bear in mind the Anti-Terrorism and Laundering Act where you may need to share information with the authorities if you suspect suspicious finance activities.

41) Link Facebook and Messenger together

Some people prefer to send you messages quickly via messenger rather than opening their email inbox and dictating an email. Having messenger is convenient and you can reply relatively quickly off your smart phone. Notifications are instantaneous so you can reply within minutes of receiving a message.

CHAPTER TWELVE

Troll Management Expert

1) Put up a Legal Pages

Whether you are designing a landing page or a website always put a disclaimer and add your terms and conditions as-well as privacy policy's onto your page. If you are managing a Facebook Page or Group make your terms and conditions part of your business Clearly state the things you will not tolerate and the consequences of the actions of the beholder. Be professional at all times and do not give people room to misbehave.

2) Closely and regularly monitor every posts made by subscribers

People around the globe can make posts on your Facebook page or blog or You Tube channel, consider your setting before allowing people to comment. With Facebook you can block people who are abusive. Be vigilant with peoples remarks.

3) Check your multimedia channels 'regularly'

Set notifications and check your viewers comments regularly. Set a CTP (Critical Time Path) that is convenient to you.

4) Consider hiring someone to manage your business.

Sometimes we do not have time to do everything ourselves and with this in mind comments may fall between the gaps. Therefore it is important that if you cannot do it yourself consider asking a friend or family member to help you out. Failing that there are companies that can manage your platforms for a nominal fee,

5) Delete derogatory comments and spam

There is no pleasing some people in this world and some will deliberately try to discredit you. Be on your guard and respond professionally preferably in a private message, after all you do not want to hang out your dirty laundry in public so to speak. These people are the detractors they just want to say bad things. Never take things personally and whenever possible delete derogatory comments. The same goes with people that spam you with unrelated garbage. Be on the ball as your image is what makes people trust you to do business with.

7) Decline to engage in argument

There are some people in this world that will attempt to provoke you into answering back. If you want to resolve an issue use private messaging and do not answer back publicly. Some people usually trolls do not have anything better to do and will want to make you to look bad. Avoid entering into arguments and delete negative messages whenever possible even going as far as reporting the person. You must be professional.

8) Use Etiquette

Some people will ask you questions through posts and

comments. Regardless if they are polite, aggressive, pushy, or just trying to annoy you, it is necessary that you answer them politely. If the comments start to get out of hand remark you will be contacting them via private message and always stand your ground by saying that all comments will be reviewed by management and no further comments will be allowed. Do not argue. Simply provide the answer to their question and decide if you want to block or report the individual. A detractor will sometimes ask a question that will attract the attention and interest of your subscribers. If you do nothing, your subscribers will think that you are avoiding the question and that you are hiding something. Do not cause doubt in an unanswered question . Let your subscriber know that you care about your business and that you want to resolve any issues that have arisen. Therefore you must answer the question thoroughly so there is no room for argument and end your remark with no further questions will be allowed.

9) Ban Abusive Users

Depending on the severity of the remarks will determine the call of action you may choose. You can either simply warn an abusive user, however if he/she is continually breaking your terms and condition and policies (e.g. posting hate comments), you may need to take the appropriate course of action in order for it not to continue and cause bad publicity.

CHAPTER THIRTEEN

TWITTER

1) Create and manage a good follower/following ratio

If you use Twitter as a personal account consider creating a business account . If you are following more people than the number of people that are following you especially if you have a business account. There should always be more people that follow you.

2) Entice followers

As with every other social media platform ask people that you know to follow you on Twitter, they could be relatives, employees, friends, and friend of friends. Then when you have generated a few followers, start commenting on other peoples tweets. If you do this regularly without spamming you will most probably get the person or the company following you.

3) Be choosy on who you follow

Only follow Companies and CEOs that matter and fit into

you niche you are trying to promote. If your domain portfolio consists of Horse Racing Domain Names consider following equestrian syndication business's.

4) Maintain a professional approach

Twitter is a prompt way to say a few words quickly. Be professional and informative and do not mix business with pleasure. Your personal opinion does not matter but your professional one does.

5) Be unrelenting in replying

Yo do not want to look pompous by refraining from replying to the questions of your followers. Unlike Facebook, Twitter puts more highlight on replies. Be professional with your replies.

6) Use your company brand

Publish your company name and logo on your twitter account. It shows you are a business and that you are trustworthy it also isolates your page from possible imposter's.

7) Connect to Popular Twitter Group

Decide what business you wish to follow do not choose random companies choose businesses that are related to your domain name niche. If you are selling a domain name related to diamonds for example for example follow jewellers or mining companies and their CEOs.

8) Ban Trolls

As with me mentioning in my Facebook article you will find displeased people that are disgruntled for what ever reason do not add fuel to the fire when some throws a lighted match, be polite and courteous and try to resolve the issue quickly and professionally do not engage in lengthy discussions, cut the person off short and consider blocking or reporting them depending on the gravity of the situation. People may talk about you. Scan your name and see what comes up .

Be vigilant and check what people are saying. If you detect any libellous comments report the person or persons to Twitter Admin. Do not engage in lengthy comments that may attract negative reactions. Give the person the benefit of the doubt and allow them to explain the issue that concerns them. If however they are just spouting out nonsense stop them in their tracks and delete anything that is slanderous. Stay clear of controversial topic especially, religion, politics and race.

9) Multiple accounts

If you choose to have multiple accounts for every individual domain name you promote be careful of the information you share with your audience. Either you stay generic and consistent right across the board or you Tweet on the individual account on the subject of the matter. Keep your personal account separate to your business accounts.

10) Consistent Announcements

Use the power of social media and announce promotions and events across all platforms at the same time avoid inconsistencies. So if you need to announce a competition or a discount sale promotions for example do it on all the same time.

11) Use a moderator

Allow one person to manage your social media accounts and your blog posts to prevent inconsistencies, whilst freeing up your time so that you can market your domain names.

12) Proofread

Check your spelling and your grammar. Check and double check your articles, no one likes typos and it does not look professional. Be a perfectionist, no matter how good you might be or how careful you are, people make mistakes, we are only human after all.

13) Share your social media accounts

You can create icons on your blog and on your website, you can mention tweets on your LinkedIn profile and on your Facebook page with links directly to the articles.

14) Report growth of other social media platforms

Tell your viewers and subscribers how your other social media accounts are doing. This will entice them to subscribe to your other accounts. In your Twitter account for example, say something like: "Our Facebook page hit its first 100,000 likes after running a competition which was won by Anne Smith from Slough. Get people engage with the hope that they may win a competition next time you decide to run one. Also you could write something simple as in your Twitter account for example, you may Tweet "check out our Facebook page as well". Some subscribers may be too lazy to check out your other accounts. Help them out by providing a link to your URL of your subdomain page of the social media platform.

CHAPTER FOURTEEN

Search Engine Optimization

The internet has evolved so much it is the number one research, shopping tool on the planet. In today's world of technology we rely on the internet for just about anything including connecting with friends and family to business networking and marketing. The World Wide Web is no longer a luxury and more a necessity in life to educate and prosper. More and more business are turning online to save costs with the traditional bricks and mortar method and can reach wider audiences far quicker.

Potentially one can make a lot of money on the internet with the right tools and knowledge. Marketers use the Internet to help drive traffic to businesses. The internet is a global phenomenon.

One needs to have a little experience in marketing and SEO with basic tips and tricks of the trade helping a newly registered domain name get ranked by search engines and both established and new starter sites generate organic traffic. Furthermore you can take your product and service to the end user simply by introducing it at their GEO location rather than setting up a physical business.

Critical Time Path (CTP

1) Add Robot txt to Website/blog/landing page
2) Add Sitemaps to Website/blog/landing page
3) Add Href Tags to Website/blog/landing page
4) Add Metatags to Website/blog/landing page
5) Add HTML Tags to Website/blog/landing page

6) Set up Google Analytic

7) Google Webmaster Search Console – Add Property

8) Google Webmaster Search Console – Verify Property

9) Google Webmaster Search Console – Crawl Property

10) Google Webmaster Search Console – Fetch as Google

11) Create a Google Business Page

12) Verify Google Business Page

13) Google Tag Manager

14) Google Maps

15) Upload to Search Engines

16) Ping Website/blog/landing page

17) Canonicalization - Choose how you want your url to appear

18) Check to see if Website/blog/landing page is mobile friendly

19) Create Social Media Pages

20) Check to Website/blog/landing page in all browsers

22) Add Terms & Conditions to Website/blog/landing page

23) Add Privacy Policy (GDPR) to Website/blog/landing page

24) Add Flavicon to Website/blog/landing page

25) List your Website/blog/landing page to all Business Directories

26) Google Brand Suite

27) Google Plus

28) Add Keywords into header and content of Website/blog/landing page.

29) Set up and Configure SSL Certificate Update site to use HTTPS - Code

30) Get more traffic use www.meetedgar.com

31) Get more traffic use www.subscribers.com

32) Get more traffic use www.ubersuggest.com

33) Get more traffic use www.typeform.com

34) Get more traffic use www.leadquizzes.com

35) Optimize Alt tags

36) Optimize size of images on website low resolution.

SEO Traffic Generation Tips

SEO (search engine optimization) is extremely important in order to be ranked by search engines and to generate traffic to the website you are marketing..There are basically three basic elements to SEO keywords, links and content. Consider keywords, links and content as the three musketeers of successful SEO.

Keywords are essential throughout your website, marketing and advertising, including keywords in your title of your domain and homepage, your subheadings and in your links.

Link wheels help with ranking your website and to show good authority. Google respects that the more times you are linked and have backlinks from respected site the quicker and higher up the ladder you will go.

Adding new original content or constantly updating your site or blog is another way a reaching number one.

Optimizing html tags and HREF, meta tags also plays an important role in SEO. Sitemaps and Google Analytics help you monitor where your traffic is coming from and how often even precise to what time of day and what browser and device was used. You can even see what IP addresses were used.

Also consider that images need Alt tag descriptions so that

they can also help attract traffic to your website.

Search Engines use algorithms that monitor yor website and some sites get banned if they do not consider the rules that the search engines expect you to adhere to.

Search engine optimization (SEO) is an essential aspect of marketing a website.

If a website has not been properly optimized, the search engines will not find it and if the search engines do not find the website then potential customers cannot find the site either. It is important that the website is designed for the search engine in mind as much as the customer in mind.There is a lot of information about search engine optimization on a variety of mediums. There are websites that "specialize" in providing free information about search engine optimization. There are companies that promise specific rankings within the search engine process. There is information floating on the internet that shows algorithms that have been used since the beginning of the search engine development.

All of this information can make it very confusing for a person to find and use the proper methods for search engine optimization in regards to their personal website or their business websites. What is important to remember, that just as computers change every few months, so too do the details for search engine optimization. The current methods that the search engines use to find a website are speculative, but not exact. There is no guaranteed method of getting a website at the very top of the potential list.

It is the job of the webmaster to continually change the site to reflect the change in the way that the search engine looks for the websites.

I

This can be reorganizing the site map, adding new content and changing the keywords that are used in the website to reflect what people are frequently searching for. This is a continual job, but with the work comes the pay off as more people find the website and purchase from it.

Why It Is Important

Search engine optimization, or SEO, is very important because without this optimization, the website will not be found by those who are surfing the Internet.

Most people fail to search beyond the 2nd page of website listings when they look for a keyword or product. The higher on the list of relevant websites the website is the better chance it has for being clicked on and viewed by the potential customer. Another reason that it is important to search engine optimize a website is to make it stand out from the other websites that might be selling the same product.

By constructing the website in a search engine friendly manner, it can mak more sense to the customer and to the individuals who are looking for the sites.

Search engines themselves are non-human and function using algorithms, so by finding the right system and processes for search engine optimization, the website will be able to fulfil all of the potential needs of the customers as well as bring in more traffic.

By performing regular search engine optimization techniques on the website, the website owner can find and correct any errors that may be on the website.

These errors can cause the website not to function appropriately, and can leave customers frustrated and unwilling to return to the website.

The process of search engine optimization can also help to identify dead links and where new content is needed. If there is a constant stream of new content, there will be something for the search engine to sort through and latch onto in regards to fulfilling the requests of the searcher. This new content can also cause people who have been at the website to pay more attention to the website even when not using the search engine. This can be done by making the website one of the favourites and by returning to the site on a regular basis.

How To Use SEO

Using search engine optimization techniques is not a simple process. This is always changing and many people find that they have difficulty keeping up with the search engine optimization changes. Luckily there are a few things that do not change in the search engine algorithms. These things may be used in a different way than they have previously been used, but they are still used by the search engines to find, sort and assign order to the websites on the Internet.

One of the best things to use for search engine optimization is keyword optimization. These are words that people use to search for items on the Internet.

The keyword is simply a word that is used in natural sentence methods that the search engine is able to latch onto and assign a code to. The more keywords there are used, the more the search engine registers the website, but if it is overly saturated, it can work the opposite way.

Tags are another common way to mark an article or website for search engine optimization. This method highlights different words for the search engine and makes them easier for the program to find. The tags do not need to be used in a natural way within the wording of the website, but rather can be listed along the side or under the text of a website.

HTML titles are the titles of the website that the search engine looks at. This is not necessarily the title of the website itself. Setting this title can be a little tricky, but once the process has been mastered, it can greatly increase the traffic to the website. Most often the title is really another set of keywords.Site descriptions and blogs are additional texts that help to identify a website and provide room for the keywords. Simply knowing what these items are can help to optimize a website, although it is much more effective to know how to use these different tools appropriately. That will be discussed immediately as each of the tools is described in depth and using them is explained. There will be samples as well, making learning the search engine optimization process that much easier.

Keywords

Keywords are the words that people use to search for a website. They place these words in the search bar of the search engine and once they hit go, the search engine works to identify these words throughout the domain names, headers and content of various websites.

Keywords can be used in a couple different ways. Keywords can be used in a natural manner in the context of the website text. This is the preferred method of keyword usage and it is also the most effective manner. This helps to ensure that the people viewing the website find what they are looking for and are not likely to click out quickly which would show as an exit from the website, which will hurt the SEO ratings

The keywords can also be used in a tagging method where they are all clumped together, creating a large number of keywords but no content. This is considered an unethical method of using keywords and it can hinder the website more than it can help the website because most search engines are programmed to detect and ignore this type of keyword entry.

Keywords should be used in the HTML and the standard title for the website.

This usage of the keyword within the titles will help people to feel more confident about viewing the website. The keywords that are used in the titles also help to ensure that the search engines find the websites with little difficulty. Be sure to use the keywords in a very fluid and natural manner when putting them into the title. The title should not be just the keywords.

One of the important things to remember about keywords is that they do not have to be exact for the search engines to find them. There are many people who are not able to spell what they are looking for, and the search engines will
approximate for the searcher. The search engine will also notice words that are close together, but not necessarily adjacent to each other.

Examples:

The searcher types in "homes" the search engine will search for "homes" as well as "home". This is a single word search engine query and it will result in many different websites. The searcher who types in "homes for sale" will receive information about "home for sale" and "homes for sales".The searcher will also find "homes for cheap sale and "homes not for sale" which are negative keywords as well, since those phrases have the words they are looking for, but there is a word between them.

The keywords are not case sensitive. The search engines do not recognize a difference between a capitalized word and one that is not. The search engines also do not notice words that are italic or bold any faster than the notice wordthat have not had the font or format altered. This used to be the case, but it is no longer recognized as a means of search engine optimization.

There are also two different forms of keywords. There are the short tail and the long tail keywords. To differentiate the two types of keywords, the short tail keywords are those that include only a few words.

Meanwhile long tail keywords are those keywords that include full questions or a series of words. Both of them garner different responses from the search engines and the websites should be prepared for either type of keyword queries.

Short Tail:

Riding a Bike, Hair Salons, Designer Handbags

Long Tail:

How to Ride A Bike, Best Hair Salons In Cardiff, where to buy real designer handbags.

The long tail search engine keywords tend to provide users with a very exact type of website that answers that specific question or statement. These long tail websites may not get as much traffic as the short tail keywords, but they do provide better quality content for the user.

Tags

Tags are words that the search engines find and latch onto similarly to keywords.

Tags are often not incorporated into the text of the website, but are attached to it though the use of a computer program. The tags do not necessarily includewords that are used in the article or text, but they can be words that describe the text. These tags can also provide link backs to other advertising sites and can help to bring in more traffic based on the back site.

Tags can be manually entered into the website. They can also be automatically handled through a variety of programs that are offered by the website hosting companies. One of the most common tagging programs is "Tag the Web" and it is offered by WordPress.com. This program highlights and "tags" words that are commonly used in the search engine process.

No matter how tags are placed on the website, they have become one of the single most important aspects to search engine optimization. They are still behind the use of keywords, but they are working their way up in importance.

Most blogs and sites have a multitude of tagged words, even though they may only have a few keywords that are used frequently.

HTML Titles

HTML titles are titles that the search engine looks at in order to determine if the website has relevant information for the searcher. It is important to remember that the search engine is not human and has no emotion; therefore it is not going to care about how flashy the title is. What the search engine cares about is whether the HTML title has the keywords that it is searching for.

HTML titles are very important for the search engine and have a limit of how many characters that are considered valid and important. Most search engines do not look beyond the first 120 characters of the title. They also tend to ignore punctuation, so placing commons, periods or other punctuations takes away from the number of characters available to use keywords in.

HTML titles are not typically visible to the person checking for the websites. Instead, this person sees the site title and the site description and makes a judgment call based on this information. In rare cases, depending upon the search engine, the HTML title can be seen, so it is important to use the keywords in a sentence or title structure.

Site Descriptions

Site descriptions are very important aspects of search engine optimization. When a site description is written, it should feature each key word at least once in natural use. This site description is used by the search engine to determine what the site is about at a mathematical level. The description is also used by the searcher as a means of deciding which website to read.

The site description therefore needs to be very interesting and relevant to the website. It is suggested that the description is written like a teaser for the website. The keywords should be in the description, as should any tagging program. This way the search engine has more that it can focus on to identify and rank the website.

Getting Help With SEO

The search engine optimization process is very complicated. With the processes constantly changing, it is not common for people to need a little help in optimizing their websites so that they are able to get the most traffic possible. There are many different companies and individuals who do understand the process an who are willing to assist a person with the website for a payment.

SEO Companies

Search engine optimization companies are the most cost effective means for optimizing a website because this is what they specialize in and they are able to do more websites faster due to a dedicated team. The downside to this method of optimization is that it often lacks the personal touch that the other methods of obtaining search engine optimization assistance can provide. Often this company is able to guarantee so many hits on the website per month.

Website Building Groups

Website building groups offer to professionally search engine optimize the website. This is often done free of charge when the company builds the website for the customer. The web building groups will set the customer up with initial search engine optimization traits for the site, but it will be up to the customer to maintain these components, such as the blog and website page information.

These website building companies will guarantee so many hits for the first few months of the website, but after that there are no promises as to the number of hits. **One.com** is one such web hosting and web building website that offers this.

Independent Contractors

Independent contractors and SEO content companies, such as the contractors on Elance.com and Guru.com, provide content for the websites that is designed to be picked up by the search engines. This content can include the blogs, ne articles, promotional work, and they may even host blogs on their other sites that provide links to the website. These businesses often do not give any guarantees as to the hits, but they do provide more information for the readers.

How to Chart SEO Success

Charting SEO success can be done in a couple different ways. There should be a chart on each backdoor operation of a website that shows how many hits the website got and what the searched keywords were. Some free companies

withhold this information for those websites that have been upgraded, but most companies allow this information to be viewed. The different blogs and article can also be tracked to see which ones are bringing in the most traffic. This can show where changes need to be made, which keywords are being searched for the most and how to better the website.

50 Things to do

1) HOOTSUITE.COM

Managing multiple social media accounts is sometime time consuming and if you can't find anyone to do it for you and you don't have the time to do it yourself, it can leave your situation slightly difficult. Therefore this Handy tool allows you to do the task with more ease. Sign up and use Hootsuite to manage all your social media accounts in one place. You can pre-program Hootsuite to make blog posts and Tweets quickly. However you have to prepare the messages in advance yourself so it is not 100% automated you still have to do a bit of work. Hootsuite.com offers a free service. The features available are limited but most businesses manage well. The free account offers the following features: manage 5 social profiles, use quick reports, use message scheduling, have 2 RSS feeds.

On the other hand If you are a user with several different social media accounts than the regular 'Joe Blogs', you might need a paid service. The paid Hootsuite service offers the following additional features: control unlimited profiles, use analytics reports, use Google analytics integration, use Facebook insights integration, have unlimited RSS feeds, have 2 free users.

2) Cross Referencing brand mentions

Sometimes a subscriber or a commenter might inconspicuously mention other brands on your page. Track this activity and see what your subscribers comments are all about. It could be that they are comparing companies or recommending ones.

3) Analytic reporting

This will make it easier for you to analyze how well your social media account is doing. Reports like traffic flow will be very useful to you.

4) RSS feeds

Use RSS feeds for automated articles in your posts. RSS Feeds are a type of news feed which allows users to aggregate updates to online content in a standardized, computer-readable format. These news feeds can, for example, allow a user to control and keep track of many different websites on one single widget that allows you to auto-update your social media accounts via news feed or from your blog.

5) Match writing style with audience

When composing your articles take into consideration your audience. Are they young or old, what location are they in, are they conservative or outgoing, are they sensitive to topics of discussion? Consider all elements before writing your articles. Consider also how you write your articles do you have an active tone that makes use of action words. Instead of saying 'If you buy this domain name…, be assertive and say instead "Buy this domain name…". This style of speech encourages readers to take action. Its gentle persuasion, whilst using direct speech.

6) Using Capitalization

Too many capital letters in a sentence is unsightly and is the equivalent to shouting, however if you want words to stand out you can highlight them not only **Bold** lettering and Italic, underlined but Capitalization of important words to make a message or blog post more noticeable. So instead of simply posting "Save up to 100 USD when you buy this domain name, capitalize your keywords to look like **"SAVE up to 100 USD when you BUY this DOMAIN NAME"**.

7) Get help and Outsource

Not all people can write content that is meaningful, that's why there are services on the web where content writers create informative articles on your behalf. They are mainly freelancers working on gigs and aswell as previously mentioned you can find them on www.fiverr.com www.freelancer.com you can also try www.odesk.com Make sure that there person you outsource your work understands the job you do and what you want from the project.

8) Competitors

Always be ahead of the completion and monitor what your competitors are up to. Be creative and always show quality in your promotions. Always do it better. If you cant do the advertising yourself then hire someone that can. Be unique in your posts, videos and promotions.

9) Set goals

When monitoring your competition analyse what they are doing and set goals to be better than them. If for example you have 1000 subscribers and your competitor has 10,000, then your goal is to get another 9,000 subscribers, by what ever means possible and it can be done as I pointed out previously. It can be done but you need the drive to achieve your goals no one can do it for you.

10) Attract your competitors subscribers

Contact your competitors subscribers with a message or a link to a useful article or video. If they find it helpful they too will subscribe to you.

Learning from your competitors

11) Analyse which of your competitors posts get more response

Study your competitors posts and analyse why those posts have gone viral. Apply the same principal to your posts, that way if you do it better you will without a doubt reap the rewards.

12) Avoid making the same mistakes

Go through your competitors website, landing page, blog or social media page see what looks unsightly and avoid making the same mistakes. I for one wont mention the company but my competitor only changed their website theme colours to match mine. I thought I must be doing something right if this company whom I assumed where bigger than me went to the trouble of re-designing their website to look like mine.

13) Monitor future events

Most companies announce their future plans on social media keep in touch with their proposals so that you can also do something that can attract business but better. Check out how fast your competitors are growing. Obviously not all companies advertise this such as myself but you can get information from the governments websites where they hold annual tax returns for limited companies and list this information publicly. You can then see the turnover of any particular company.

14) Replying to blog posts

When you reply to posts whether it is social media or a blog post always mention your company and send a link. If your domain name is long winded you can use Google URL shortener to send a quick link. Do not spam

15) Make individual accounts for each of your domain names

This will benefit your future clients whilst helping you be professional with the promotion of you domain names. Having individual social media pages will not only be the foundations to the start of business which you are potentially promoting but you also will be advertising your domain name for a buyer/investor.

Although these accounts are obviously not an actual business as you need an investor for that they are in fact dummy accounts that can be developed into a real business providing your domain name sells.

INFLUENCER

16) Mentors and Role Models

See who in the industry is well known, read about their achievements. Contact these people for advise, follow them on social media and learn from the experts.   I have my favourite few people that I am connected with on LinkedIn. If your stuck and you need a second opinion this is by far the best place to start. If these people are connected with you and you reach out to them 9 times of 10 they will reply back to you.

17) Learn from the Leaders

Educate yourself why the people that you choose as your Mentors succeeded and try to follow their business plan. Obviously you cannot copy it step by step but you can have an idea what they have done to be where they are. Apply their techniques to your business. Take note of the differences between your company and your role model company even if your company is in the same industry.

SURVEYS Getting Information

18) Send questionnaires

Offer a survey in exchange for either monetary compensation or a discount on the users next purchase. Say for instance you want business's to tell you their vulnerabilities and offer them either money back on the next time they buy from you or give a discount on you product or service, for example if a company needs more traffic to their website after you have established this from the survey you received offer them £100 off their next website or 10% of the next domain name they purchase from you. People are more inclined to fill out a survey if they have something back in return.

19) Ask your clients for their opinions

Never be afraid of asking for opinions even from your own clients. If you establish a rapport with your client you can ask them for their opinion for example about a competitor you are analysing to see if they would approve if you did something similar. I speak to my clients which are all over the world. I give them my time of day so they feel confident to just phone me to ask questions and visa versa. I prefer contacting my clients by email it is less intrusive and if I want their opinion I usually get what I am looking for.

Doing Surveys Right

20) Short Surveys

People like myself for instance do not like to fill time consuming lengthy surveys. Keep your surveys short and viewers will most likely be willing to participate. Also give incentives for filling out the survey. The same goes for newsletters if you offer a viewer a free e-book they are more likely to take part. Keep the questions to a minimum. Also keep your choices to a maximum of three.

21) Pin/Star

Pin and Star feature is available in Facebook. You can 'star' or 'pin' a post to make it more visible. When you post a survey, you should either make it a Starred post of a Pinned Post to get more visitors.

Survey Advertising

22) Write in header in Facebook

In your Facebook account announce you are holding a survery and write it in the header, which is located Facebook group account, this is the 'About' page. Write something like: "We are currently holding a survey please take a minute to fill it in and you will receive xyz.

23) Website or Blog

If you use Google Analytics (highly recommended) You can safely say people are looking at your website or blog Therefore if you announce you are holding a survey on Facebook people may go to check it out, alternatively integrate it into your website or blog.

24) RSS feed

You can preset your RSS page to publish a reminder that tells your viewers to join your survey.

26) Newsletters

A newsletter is the alternative to an online magazine, it normally is free of charge and is usually a page long full of information and backlinks to other news articles. Encourage your viewers to join and be up to date with all the latest industry news, promotions and trends. This is also a good idea to promote your domain portfolio. So that your subscribers see what you have for sale. Offer an incentive to join.

MARKETING

27) Announce your promotions or sales in advance

Sometimes announcing a promotion or sale a week in advance helps get people to share your news with other people so that your able to get full coverage.

28) Use teaser words

By announcing a week in advance you could entice people to spread the word of a promotion or sale coming their way by saying something like: "we have a special surprise for our customers next week" this will inevitably get your subscribers curious even telling their friends.

29) Stand out in the crowd

To highlight marketing techniques consider using videos, images, sound clips, slide shows, as well as making your header bold and big.

30) Look after your loyal customers

Do not just send your loyal customers generic newsletters reach out personally and tell them in a private message you are informing them of up and coming event, promotions or sales. This makes your customer feel special.
Up-selling/Cross-selling

31) Up-sell/Cross-sell

So you have a customer that wants you to broker their domain name. You have done outbound marketing but you can also upsell them a seo landing page not a template that floats in cyber space but a one page website that is optimized to its full potential. There fore if you tell your customers in advance of the services you have to offer it won't be a blow to the system when you send them promotions.

32) Tell people why they need it

Explain to your subscribers why it would benefit them to have a one page developed website as not only it will generate traffic for their domain name it will also generate traffic for your future investor, as well as making your domain more valuable.

33) Give Saving Incentives

If you are a website developer or are affiliated with one, tell people how much they will save if they buy an up-sell. Give a deadline that it will be only available for the next 24- 48 hours.

Show a visual portfolio

34) Upload logos

Capturing your investors imagination usually helps with a logo for the domain name your are promoting. People tend to look at images rather than text.

35) Be descriptive

Write about the domain name and what industry it would fit and why. Explain how many times it is searched for per month and the cost of the keyword. Calculate how much and investor would save in PPC advertising if they where to acquire your domain name.

36) Update your inventory

There are many places available that can store your domain names and integrate them with a payment gateway. I personally like www.ecwid.com and they even list 10 items for free before you have to upgrade they are also easy to use and have customer support if you need their help for whatever reason. You can even have a Facebook shop which I think is quite cool. Your updates are instantaneous.

37) List the categories of the Industries

Lets say for example you are selling Club domains, your industry categories would be hospitality, night, clubs, youth centres or even organizations. By having categories the user will quickly find your domain name.

38) Be clear your listing is not finished

Sometimes you need more time to finish your listings hence I say POA and description coming soon, that way I can come to the listing later to finish it off. By saying price on application you are giving the viewer to make a the decision to enquire and even make an offer.

GLOBAL LANGUAGE

39) Translation

Some viewers do not speak your language, integrate a translation widget into your store so that people can quickly translate your listings. Google have their own widget code that you can embedded. Facebook already offers this option. However, you cannot control what language your subscribers will use when they post a message on your wall unfortunately. Also remember USA Engish Spelling may be slightly different to UK English.

40) Simplified English

Your posts and your listing should be user friendly. Not everyone understands complex words, therefore it is imperative that people from all walks in life will understand what you are trying to say. It also translates better when you have simplified text especially when you put it through a translation widget. Do not over complicate your sentences and keep it simple.

CORRECT TIMING

41) Timing is crucial

Consider when people are most likely to read your posts. CEOs have a busy work schedule and do not have time to open LinkedIn for example, the same goes for people in work that may not be able to use their Mobile phone (Cell phone). Your posts will eventually get saturated amongst every ones else's if you do not time it perfectly. Not everyone works 7 days a week so think about Sundays where people are resting and surfing the internet for their own pleasure.

42) Global timing

Time differences also make your job that much harder especially that you should not be repetitive with your postings. Decide a time of day where all viewers will see your post and at the most only post twice, once in the morning and once at night. Re-posting posts generally is not a good idea as people do not want to read old news. If however you want your listing to be seen perhaps by more people, make a similar post and ask your subscribers to share the post to get added exposure.

43) Multiple posts

If you have multiple domain names you wish to share with your audience do not send them all at once as some of the messages might not get noticed. Have a timeline and plan when to post each post.

44) Timing your replies

Let other subscribers add to the conversation first before replying immediately this way you are establishing your plan for response that will please your readers. Do not take days to respond as this will look unprofessional, instead give a few hours so that people can add their own comments in.

45) Timing follow-ups

When you send an email give some time for people to read it the same goes with traditional mail and allow them to respond, even add in your email or letter that you will follow-up in 3 days for instance. Do not send out newsletters immediately when some one has signed up as a subscriber as this looks like your desperate. Give people time to respond.

46) Your profile

Be careful what you want the public to read and change your profile with the seasons. People like images, change your profile pictures to a Festive one at Christmas. Have a Christmas banner with your logo. Write what is fitting for your description and don't allow trolls to twist your words.

I will give you an example of something that happened to me most recently. I use a link-wheel to drive traffic to my main website, so even though I have been established since 1993 my websites have not.

By having fairly new domain names gave the impression that my business has not been around for very long but if the troll had bothered to dig deeper he would have found that I have been around for a very long time.

What caused the confusion was I happened to write on all my domain extensions that I have over 25 years experience and this troll happened to point out the domains were not registered for that length of time.

In my defence I had to explain myself of which the troll continued to make derogatory comments and tried discrediting me. I have since updated my profile and have blocked this individual. Remember sometimes writing less about yourself and directing your audience to your website gives a better impression and opinion. Lesson learnt.

47) Taking down a post

Sometimes it is necessary to take down posts, although on some forums it may not be that easy and you will have to speak to the webmaster for that, but generally speaking if you are in control of your own account you can basically do it yourself. Consider carefully taking down information that can be useful to people in future.

48) Timing of surveys

People are more suscptible to agreeing to taking a survey when they are in the mood, usually after work or after a holiday, they may even fill out surveys on pay days usually if you offer a discount incentive in exchange for their information.

CLEVER TRICKS

49) Keep this secret
Web developers and internet marketers, use dummy accounts to make reviews on your services and products.

Use dummy accounts to make positive reviews and start conversations. Dummy accounts should each use a unique email for registration. Also, each dummy account must have a private profile (cannot be viewed) to hide the fact that they are in fact dummy accounts. Use these accounts to write positive responses to your wall posts. Also, use these accounts to give positive reviews to the products/services that you advertised. Sound Believable. Do not go overboard with your ratings, people can spot a dummy account if you are not natural. Outrageously sounding reviews are not believable. Also, they will raise the suspicion of your other subscribers and other onlookers. Make sure that the positive reviews you posted using your dummy accounts all sound natural.

50) Hire a content writer

Sometimes it is time consuming to write reviews about your own products and services so outsourcing the work to someone else who is a professional content writer may save you writing repetitive comments that can look re-written. As I have mentioned before www.fiverr.com whom I am not affiliated with offer this service for as little as $5.00. Try not to use the same writers too many times as you will be back with the same problem of regurgitated information. There is no harm to ask your friends, family and co-workers to right glowing reviews. This makes your reviews look original and authentic.

FINAL TIPS
Your social media is part of your link-wheel.

A link-wheel has multiple extensions branching out from your default website. Keep in mind that search engine optimization includes cogs in a wheel that give traffic from multiple directions. Hence backlinks to your website help your website run just like you would expect an engine to do. Social media platforms, forums, bogs and classified ads drive organic traffic to your website/ landing page. These backlinks are an extension of your company. It embodies your company.

Your company's social media accounts are separate from you

Do not use your own personal social media accounts set up business accounts that deliver a professional message. Keep in mind that your company's social media accounts represents your company and not you. As the moderator, it can be hard not to display your own personality. But you must train yourself to be neutral.

Social media can be a powerful tool, providing it is the right hands, it can propel any business to the top. With the right strategies, a company might see a significant increase in sales within a short period of time. With the right moderators, a company can gain significant popularity from the public. Just as quickly social media can expand your business into sometime big it can just as quickly destroy your reputation. Be very careful in the use of social media. More often than not it is not very often that a company wrongly uses a social media account, so providing you follow the rules you should not go wrong.

Websites are very difficult and complicated to manage in terms of search engine optimization. Although you can design a website on many hosting platforms for free or at a very low cost, this will not get you on the first page of any search engine without the right knowledge and tools. As I mentioned at the beginning of this Chapter, I use a set of rules to optimize my websites, follow my steps and you too will be found for your search terms and keywords whilst at the same time also generating organic traffic for your future investor.

CHAPTER FIFTEEN

Valuation / Appraisals

So you have an average of how many impressions you get per month but not everyone who sees your listing is necessarily going to click on your website. The average click through ratio is only 2% of the impressions. I then divide 2% by the original figure of the average searches per month, I then times that figure by 12 months to get an overall price how much an end user would have to pay a search engine for advertising.

I also take into account how old the domain name is and if it has a website associated with it and if it has been optimized and ranking well and how much traffic it is / has generating (ed). I then sit down and work out how much I am willing to sell the domain for based on my figures and how much the end user would potentially save per annum if they were to purchase the domain.

Bear in mind that sometimes a low search volumn does not necessarily mean that your domain name is worthless, if the keyword(s) have value to the content that can be developed this could in fact increase the value of your domain. Here is an example say for instance the word **'diamond'** had a low search volumn (even though in reality the search is 301,000 times per month at a cost of £3.99) but just imagine if it had zero searches.

But your domian was **www.500ctdiamond.forsale**, you would in fact have to calculate how much such a diamond of this calibre would cost in reality and what type of company would sell it and determine the cost of the domain by these factors.

I also sometimes include a Website with SEO, Marketing and Business Consulting, Trademark Registration and Company Formation to add more value to the domain and may even offer to lease the domain or spread the cost over 12 to 60 months. To eliminate the headache of renewals I will renew the domain name five years in advance and notify my client if they are not developing a website or leasing the domain name with me, they will have to renew their domains in five years time at a cost of £xx..xx per domain.

I am meticulous when it comes to contracts. I do not offer any service without a signed agreement.

www.startbrand.co.uk has legal documentation that you can have on application free of charge.

Another scenario that I came across most recently was a domain name that was listed on a few networks for $1,000,000 so a domainer asks me to broker a similar one for the same price. I personally thought the domain was over priced at first until I approached the owner of the original domain advertised giving the second domainer the idea he could list it for the same price. The difference was the original seller of the first domain had a business plan included with his package whilst the second person did not, therefore the price of the domain had to be reduced significantly in order for me to list it.

Basically you need to do your research on what will you think will sell. I personally stick to generic keywords that describe your niche.

PRICING YOUR DOMAINS

Have you ever wondered why Domain Brokers do not tell you how to directly appraise your domain name? Have you noticed how they go roundabout the houses without actually telling you how to evaluate the price of the domain?

Basically they would go out of business if they spilt trade secrets as valuations are a service and if everyone knew how to value their domain names properly there would be no need to offer the service at all. Some sites charge up to $59 for one valuation of one domain name thats no 1 and no 2 some people do not even know how to appraise a domain properly and just go by previous sales to get a valuation or use bots such as 'Esitbot'.

You do not need a PHD to do a valuation you just need to be able to do the maths and as one person tried to point out that you need to issue certificates. Certificates are what an accredited company issues when you exchange money for each individual domain name appraisal service.

But where there is the internet and where there is the information and thats why I often post on my blog regularly what you should do. There is not much written about this and that is why things are about to change.

Recently I have been pondering on the thought of the hundreds of thousands of domain names that are registered daily with people who have no clue about marketing and hope to win the jackpot with their unique domain names.

From a marketing perspective if someone asked me to broker a 'NNN' domain or a 'LLL' domain, I would first have
to ask myself who would buy it and how would it be useful to the end user for Search Engine Optimization. Would the end user acquire it to sell on as a profit and possibly brand it in some way as such domain names have no value in search terms, unless they have been developed and extensively marketed so much so that search engines find the keywords using their algorithms.

It is common knowledge that Chinese investors that are buying up these domains and something came to me about one wholesaler in China who every so often has her website taken down as she sells fake handbags and clothes. She never uses keywords in her domain names and does not do any SEO for the simple reason that she can send a link directly to her customers without the authorities catching up with her. Mostly she will use scrambled made up words or acronyms i.e letters, numbers, combo. This is possibly the only reason why Chinese investors buy up such domain names as they are disposable, unless they are auspicious in some way like 8888 for instance. The counterfeit industry is a multi-billion dollar industry so buying up domain names that are less likely to be found by the authorities is to the owner of his her business, a domain name a valuable asset.

If you think about a business starting out, the first thing they will do is search to see if a domain name they have chosen is available or not. If it has been taken they will look for alternative domain extensions.

Failing that they will rebrand themselves and look for alternative names. The way to find investors is to advertise on startup sites or look for companies not ranking well on search engines in your niche or companies that are paying for advertising. I would also search classified ads for new businesses and start discussions on community forums.

Unless you have little black book of investors you can call on, your chances of selling your domain name are really slim. yes there are domain investors on social media pages and groups aswell as the popular domain marketplaces, but unless you are prepared to pay for featured listings your domain just get swollen up in a saturated market.

I'm going to be brutal here, sorry folks, but I'm not going to sugar coat things to make you feel good.

I'm going to give you an honest professional opinion. Should you take my advice is up to you.

I will first state that some domains are ridiculously over priced as people do not know what they are doing and they are just picking random numbers out of hat in the hope that some one will pay for their ridiculous prices. **People need to be aware that domains serve a purpose to help drive traffic to a business** and the best way of valuation is through working out the cost of the keyword's when paying for PPC Advertising. I have spoken to many marketing companies that are only now learning the value of keyword domains whilst others believe that the websites they manage will drive enough traffic therefore the point of purchasing an additional domain would prove worthless.

The internet has **overrated the value of some domains** and people are under the impression they can get rich quick and leave their day jobs to work on beaches or near luxury swimming pools for only a few hours each day. Some domains are not worth the money that people have spent on them. **Unless your domain names are exact match keyword's that are pronounceable,** the chances of anyone ever buying anything else is a distant unrealistic dream and nothing more. Your **keyword domain names have to flow** and not be cryptic. **Put yourself in the place of the person searching for something on the internet and type in those search terms** not acronyms, anagrams or hacks. Think like your average Joe Blogs searching for something.

Don't use hyphens or initials plus a keyword, **ONLY use exact match keywords.**I have a service that I offer, **'Contact Me Before You Buy'**, ask me if your domain is worth buying or not and I will tell you straight !!I recently read that someone invented this formula on valuing domain names. This is nothing new!! **Ask 'Google Partners' who manage 'Google Ads' how they work out budgets for campaigns. Phone Google** (You must have a Gmail account before you do and set up a Google Ads Campaign).Yet the article was published on well known business news website and how they actually made it public is beyond me.

The guy that wrote the article was only 50% correct in what he said. His statement said he had invented this formula which I find absolutely absurd and he continued to say how he finds out how many searches per month your domain generates and then multiplies that by the cost of the keyword, *he then goes on to say that you also have to multiply how many years it will take for your domain to be ranked by the search engines.*

This is ridiculous in itself as any reputable SEO Marketer who knows what they are doing should be able to get a website ranked under 12 months let alone 10 years as it was mentioned.

There would be hardly any point buying the domain in the first place if it took 10 years to be ranked and I would fire the SEO Marketer for selling me a 'DUD' Domain if that was the case.

The naivety of people who actually believe that this formula is something new are very much mistaken and gullible to believe his formula is even accurate.

The correct way of valuing of Domain Names are as follows:

1) See how many searches per month your keyword(s) generate

2) Multiply that figure my the cost of the keyword.

3) Multiply the figure by 12 months as it may take up to 12 months to get your Domain Ranked for the first page of the main Search Engines. Every year after that is what your buyer will get ROI and save in PPC advertising if they were to buy your Domain Name.

4) Divide that Figure by a click through ratio of 2% as not everyone that searches for your keywords will necessarily click on your website and this is what Search Engines Charge you for when you have PPC advertising.

5) You can also determine that some domains may have been previously developed and have been ranked for many years generating organic traffic in which you would have to analyse the analytics and multiply your PPC adverting figure by the amount of traffic your domain name fetch.

6) Finally if you have a website that either will be branded into a multi-million business and you know for definite that it is a new product or describes a niche that is unique such as for example www. 500ctbluediamond.com **(This is not a real domain name and is only used for example purposes).** Now imagine you have a jeweller who owns a 500ct Blue Diamond (which I doubt even one exists, by say for argument sake it did). The jeweller would obviously want to either advertise his diamond or try to sell it, although in the real world something like this would be auctioned off in 'Sothebys' or 'Christies' and would have PR and Media Advertising attention.

But say the jeweller did not want to use an auction house but wanted his own website dedicated to this diamond and the searches per month were 1,000 multiplied by the example I made in points 1-4 and the cost was £20 per click this would make a total of £20,000 per month times 12 months of paid advertising would leave a total of £240,000 per annum divided by 2% click through ratio would leave a total of £4,800 but the value of the diamond was £100M and the jeweller ends up selling it for £500M. You could then in theory charge a real estate commission fee of up to 6% of the valuation of that diamond not what it could sell for as there are always uncertainties in every market including auctions.

So your hypothetical asking price would be 6% of £100 Million equates to £6M in the most extreme cases of having a very unique domain name that a buyer would need in order to market their product. Otherwise stick to points (1-5) when valuing your domain names and although the free bot tools are not 100% accurate they can give you some idea which may also be useful when valuing your domain names, but should not be set in stone.

If I was to buy a domain name from a marketing perspective whereby I was acting on my clients behalf and they wanted to know how much they would save on PPC this would be my valuation and not a comparable one of a previous sale. The reason I say this because not everyone has the same budgets or buying power, it all depends on the company and on how much they are prepared to spend. Once you establish their budget for their marketing and advertising needs you can then negotiate pricing.

One has to decide what to base your valuation on. Is it the Keyword planner which calculates how much traffic you would expect to get in any given month and is an exact valuation of which if you bought the domain name you would potentially save on 'Paid Per Click Advertising' or an asking price from the seller.

The same goes if I owned a Ferrari and wanted $1M for it but it was only worth $200,000 on the books. Perhaps I would find someone that would pay me $1M. But if I was the buyer I would ask questions like how did I reach that figure in the first place and I would look at the market value that car dealers have in yearly updated books with set prices. So unless my Ferrari was encrusted with diamonds

I would most probably not find a buyer for the price I was looking to sell.

People are astute with their money, they just won't give it away for the sake of it, they will argue (barter - haggle - negotiate) to get the best prices.

At the end of the day it is down to the Buyers Budget and if its out of his/her price range they will not buy from you, so you have to give them incentives such as leasing to still try and get a sale.

With leasing I will get the buyer to sign a minimum of five year agreement in which after the five years he can buy it outright for a nominal fee. This way it is easier on the pocket. Where buy I provide a website, marketing and SEO I will work out a price to include the domain name and my services.

Before I go, a websites not only needs keywords in the Domain Name it need keywords in its content, headers and meta tags. Its not as easy as you think to simply buy a keyword domain name and hey presto,......... you have work on it and your SEO to get your domain ranked. Its not magic it takes years of practice and you need to know what your doing.

Furthermore Business's are reluctant to buy from ordinary folk. I suggest branding yourself as a business and approach them professionally by introducing yourself and explaining why they should buy your domain name. If anything I hope I have saved someone money, renewing a domain name or considering buying one that has no value at all.

CHAPTER SIXTEEN

DOMAIN HACKS & HYPHENS

Domain Hacks & Hyphens Valuation.

DOMAIN HACKS

If your wondering what this is its a short link to your main website. Will people remember to put the dot in the right

place, most probably not. Will it drive traffic to your localized area most definitely not. Will you need to do extensive PR Marketing and Multi Media Advertising, of course you will.

Will a Domain Hack benefit your business?, I don't think so.

Why do I say this....they are just accessories and nothing more they wont get you on the first page of any search engine unless you live in Libya that is or Germany as an example with the extensions .ly and .de to name a few. You will get traffic from that country as search engines use algorithms to force traffic from the location the domain is located.As an example dot com's...... businesses in the UK tend to avoid this domain extension as they will be inundated with traffic from the US and when it comes to paid per click advertising you certainly do not want the traffic from the US if you have no reason to trade there.

This will inevitably costs business's money, the same goes with Domain Hacks.

Hyphenated Domain Names

Avoid hyphens. If your domain name is two words like for example (www.renatabarnes.com), you may want to separate the words with a hyphen for readability: www.renata-barnes.com. **(These domains names do not exist in case you are wondering or if they are after I publish this book they are in no way affiliated with me :-)).**

Keep in mind these domain names are usually worthless or of little value and that the use of hyphens also strongly correlates with spammy behavior and decreases domain name readability and memorability. Not only this search engines will not recognise hyphens and will not rank your website, landing page or blog very well or even at all.

CHAPTER SEVENTEEN

Networking

Looking at network marketing as a business option is what most startup companies are doing as the implications of success are quite well documented and evident. As there are many choices available it is easy to get confused, therefore a careful study should be done to be equipped with the best information to get started.

Among the more positive aspects of the network marketing element is the entry cost that is relatively low. When compared to other startup options this platform provides less capital involvement.

The Basics

It is also a much faster way of actually getting the business started as compared to the more conventional way. There are also a lot of supporting tools that can be used without many problems as long as the right tools are identified early on in the endeavour.

Understanding that the progress of the business depends very much on the individual is also another point that could be viewed as positive.

Having control over the pace of the business growth is beneficial especially when it is in the launching stage. There is less likely to have overwhelming impact on the individual as the pace is self dictated.

This referral marketing style is quite a good tool to use as building the relationships with the customers becomes just as important as the product or service being sold.

There is also the availability of being able to reach a wider target audience through this platform choice. There is no real need for expensive advertising campaigns to reach the same desired goals.

Some statistics have also shown that the products and services being featured through this network marketing business style tend to have better quality when compared with others.

This is mainly because the survival of the business entity depends very much on the referrals it receives.

Decide On Your Passion

When faced with a lot of possible options it may be very difficult to make a choice on what would satisfactorily answer the question on what one is passionate about. One way of finding out which is the best option is to do research on what is available and currently making a success in the networking marketing world.

Deciding on things such as how much is one willing to commit to this endeavor, how long is one willing to commit in terms of a set time frame manageable, what resources are available to ensure some level of success, who would make the best customers, if the product or service being offered something that would be on interest to the masses and may more connective questions.

All these should be asked and answered in an honest fashion without hesitation or reservations. Upon gaining some insight into these areas then one can take the next step in deciding what's suitable.

Below are some areas one may want to explore in the quest towards identifying what suitable:

- Affiliate programs – a great home business option this platform allows the individual to start-up almost immediately marketing products or services from a few respected sources. Some of the elements it would require attention are the setting up of a professional looking website, understanding and choosing the best ways to direct traffic to the site and perhaps effectively working out an affiliate business tie-in.

- Creating an information product – writing e-books, subscription newsletters, creating other kinks of informational products are some of the items that this endeavour requires to make it a success. Also being able to produce quality material that can be easily sold is important.

- Creating websites – if creativity is one of the passions of the individual then this may suit his or her needs. The flexible working hours and the almost unbridled leeway given would be one of the desirable features of this type of endeavour.

Lots of people today are looking for alternative to making serious money without actually having to do the 9 – 5 office routine. Though most people fear the uncertainly of the online network marketing arena, it does have its merit and if properly understood and applied it can make for a very successful experience.

The Right Company

The important step of choosing a suitable business model and then finding the right companies to form a comfortable business liaison is the every important task to consider carefully.

Finding one's own strengths and weaknesses would also help to define the options available for a business partnership. The companies that are eventually identified according to what is passionate to the individual would then provide the launching pad for the whole exercise.

This in turn will be able to sufficiently bring about the desired effects of prosperity and hoped financial freedom.

Certain elements should be well defined before even sourcing for the right candidate that fits into the individual passion choice. These may include details such as thinking about a plan to put into motion, the budget that is comfortable to work within, a mentor with whom to either work with or follow in.

Once all the relevant information is processed then taking the step to actually start the endeavour is equally important. There is no room for procrastination one all the supporting elements are firmly in place.

It is definitely easier to work with companies that share the same ideas and projections as this will facilitate a better working relationship and the supporting internet tools can be effectively used to further support the liaison.

The advantage of tapping into an already existing target audience base is also beneficial as both parties can further extend the reach of the proposed business liaison.

Forming partnerships with other business entities is always a risky exercise to commit to. Therefore it is necessary to try and find out as much as possible about the company one is interested in forming a business liaison with before even actually going through the motions.

Do Your Homework

There are some advantages in forming a partnership and the foremost one would be to acquire a larger customer base. This coupled with the equally larger capacity to cater to this now new found large customer base will bring in the enhanced revenue earnings that are anticipated.

There are other reasons besides simply wanting to establish the financial and reputable standing of the intended partner and these may include the need to evaluate potential competitors.

Determining if the competitor is financially and business sound would then dictate the circumstances of whether the said competitor is able to expand within the current market share or whether there is a possibility of entering new markets or ventures.

Regular checks made into the backgrounds of the competitors and also the protective partners will give the individual a better and more informed view of the credit rating and progress of the said company.

This will in turn will allow the interested party to decide accordingly if the intended liaison would be a beneficial exercise to embark upon.

Poor financial standing would effectively restrict the expansion plans of a company thus making the stronger financial standing intended partner have better say in any decisions made. It would also signify the inability for the company to make any new investments into new technologies.

All these factors can then be taken into account when looking for a potential partner and these checks can easily be done as there are many companies which carry such services. Websites and links can be found and followed to facilitate the relevant background checks.

Research The Company's Leadership

The general direction and progress of a company is directly affected by the kind of leader or leaders are at the helm. There is very little doubt that the person taking the leadership role should be one who is as well informed as possible of the nature of the business and its outside effecting elements. The leader should also be able to effectively lead the team along the intended path effectively and decisively.

Who's In Charge

When conducting a researching exercise into the capabilities of a company's leadership the following are some of the important elements that should be ever present:

- The company's leadership should consist of a clear vision with a vivid picture of the intended goal everyone is working towards. Without this vision it would be very difficult to get all involved totally committed and focused in achieving the said vision.

✓ Besides having a clear vision there is also the need to work together on the same thinking and implementing processes. Getting everyone to share in and act on the same principals is what a good company leader should be able to accomplish.

✓ The company's leadership qualities should reflect the ability to communicate well within all segments of the overall working force. Communicating the vision to all levels within the company and ensuring all are of complete understanding of what is desired is important to the final accomplishments of the company.

✓ The company's leadership must also reflect the work ethics that are strong and unquestionable. This is a very important and admirable tool to inculcate and be seen as very visible. When a leader is highly respected, getting the workers to willing commit to the company's vision is not an uphill battle. Constantly inspiring everyone and keeping everyone aware of the vision of the company will eventually contribute to its unrivalled success.

Research The Company's Product Quality

Besides good leadership and management having a sound and high quality product is imperative to the **survival and** success of any company.

The service or product being sold has to be as much as possible beyond reproach. The following are some qualities or points that should be reflected the in company's product quality:

The Products

High quality products are without doubt the survival factor of any company. This particular niche should not be compromised in anyway. In fact all efforts should always be focused on maintaining this element.

Having a strong marketing department is also another instrumental element that ensures the product is always at its optimum promised levels. Adequate budgeting should be allocated to this department, second only to the advertising budget.

Maintaining the quality levels while at the same time being innovative is what will keep the product or service compatible when outside opposing factors are not favourable.

Production aspects of the company should also be able to reflect the innovative style and end product that is intended for market distribution.

Without the support of good production tools and without the constant evolving and allowance for newer more efficient methods this goal may be severely compromised.

Through the whole process of trying to stay competitive without compromising on quality, there should also be some focus on the monetary expenditure involved. Finding ways to adequately address possible increasing costs can be quite a problem is not tackled correctly. While costs are bound to escalate, product quality should never be in jeopardy of decline.

It would be an advantage to any business endeavour if there is a strong team in place to explore potential new avenues or products that could contribute positively to the overall company's revenue and image.

Where market demand is always hungry for newer and more interesting products, keeping steadfast to the old styles and product although undisputed in its capabilities would not financially benefit or grow the company.

Research The Company's Compensation Plan

Having good compensation plans is always a good and attractive feature to encourage high productivity and loyalty levels in any company. When people feel they are well taken care of then they are more like to be more committed to giving their best to the business endeavor at hand.

Understanding and acknowledging that some compensation plans generally look good on paper but are in fact very different when it comes to applying it in a practical sense.

This is of course quite a common problem and has proven to be the dominant factor in turning people away from such endeavours. Therefore one should always evaluate any proposed compensation plan properly before deciding to make the commitment.

What About The Pay

The following are some of the points worth considering when researching a company's compensation plan:

⌐ Having good compensation plans but not very good products to promote will not create the ideal circumstance to earning the desired revenue perceived. If the product line is not up to par and the individual is not adequately convinced of its touted capabilities, the sales are not going to be made and thus the compensation plan will not be beneficial.

⌐ Compensation plans should be designed as easy to understand tools. If the plan on paper looks complicated and unachievable then those interested in promoting the product will eventually lose interest in the business. Besides being easy to understand and absorb the compensation plan should also be easy to explain. Knowing the beneficial points but not being able to adequate explain them so that they appear lucrative is also self defeating.

⌐ Good compensation plans will also have proven track records that are well documented to back up the claims made. Picking companies that have sound compensation plans and that have been in business for a safe amount of time is important. Some newer companies may not have had the time frame to prove themselves yet so it may be risky taking on such entities.

Research The Company's Start Up Fees And Support

Every business endeavor involves some monetary commitment from the very onset of even thinking about it. Most people fail to take this into account and end up being frustrated when the costs are not budgeted for. Even start up fees require some planning is this can involved a sum that it non refundable. Besides this element there is also the element of adequate support provided for the new comer to the business.

What Will It Cost

The following are some points to consider when it comes to start up costs or fees:

✓ If the business entity requires a signing on fee then this is a fairly straight forward arrangement. However if the business requires further investment costs then the start up expenses angle should be explored.

✓ The start-up assets are also another point to consider. Things like cash capital, starting inventory, office equipment, furniture and the list goes on. There are elements that should be well factored into the overall budget allocations made before the business takes shape.

✓ Start-up financing is where capital investment and loan are considered. Keeping this well in control and under strict dispensing criteria is important.

When starting out in any business endeavour the supporting help available is very important. This is especially so if the business requires the advice and input of more established members.

Therefore having a good support system in place is very beneficial indeed. Below are some points to consider when searching for good support:

✓ One of the key factors to note is whether there is a comprehensive overview of the operational functions in place. This will help when there are explicit questions asked to ensure satisfactory answers are given.

✓ The support should include advice on areas identified for cost cutting or better management of budgets.

✓ Providing applicable advice on handling customers or building better customer relationships should also be part of the support provided.

Stay Up To Date On Legitimate Network Marketing Opportunities

In the quest to look for rewarding ways to making easy money, most people turn to online businesses with the hope that it will adequately address their needs. However along with a lot of legitimate business endeavors online there are also the ones that one needs to be weary of as some more often than not turn out to be scams in one form or another.

Important Decision

If one is serious in wanting to source for legitimate business opportunities, there are several reputable sites online through network marketing opportunities that can provide such information. Most of these sites are respected and don't short change their visitors as they have almost nothing to gain by doing so.

Among the various ways of identifying which kinds of business to venture into would be to use the current expertise available or the educational tools acquired over time.

Putting these to use in the form of owning a business will definitely come in useful. Also acknowledging the fact that whatever choice made is going to a huge part of the person's daily life is an important fact to consider.

The time spent on the legitimate network marketing opportunity chosen should be nothing short of what would be expected of the individual should he or she be working for a company. This initial commitment of time can then be lessened as the business takes off.

Wrapping Up

Whatever the choice made, the individual should ensure all the points from the previous topics are carefully explored as they all have connective advice leading up to this point of actually staying abreast with what's current. Keeping in touch with others in the online business platform will also enable the individual to know what is currently happening and its legitimacy tags.

CHAPTER EIGHTEEN

Email Writing & Marketing

Its suprising how many people do not know how to write emails correctly. Here's a scenario, you have done your research and you know what industry you are going to target, but the thing is you have never made contact with the companies before, so how do you get round this?

Either way phoning or emailing can be seen a cold calling or spam. I personally do not like to do business on the phone and detest telemarketers. Therefore the less intrusive way is to email. The recipient opens their inbox in their own time whilst with telephone marketing you may never get to speak to the person you wish to speak to.

Emailing is of course saves on the carbon footprint and saves money but not all emails end up in the recipients inbox straightaway until they have accepted you as trustworthy source, so in some cases your email will find itself in the junk folder.

Give yourself 5 -7 days for a recipient to contact you if they haven't proceed with writing them a traditional letter that you will unfortuantely have to be sent by post.

This way you are still not inconveniencing anyone and they can read the mail in their own time.

More often than not, email is the most common form of business communication so it's important to get it right. Although emails usually aren't as formal as letters, they still need to be professional to present a good image of you and your company.

How to write a formal email

Follow these five simple steps to make sure your English emails are perfectly professional.

>*Begin with a greeting
>*Thank the recipient
>*State your purpose
>*Add your closing remarks
>*End with a closing

Begin with a greeting

Always open your email with a greeting, such as "Dear Lillian". If your relationship with the reader is formal, use their family name (eg. "Dear Mrs. Price"). If the relationship is more casual, you can simply say, "Hi Kelly". If you don't know the name of the person you are writing to, use:

"To whom it may concern" or "Dear Sir/Madam".

Thank the recipient

If you are replying to a client's inquiry, you should begin with a line of thanks. For example, if someone has a question about your company, you can say, "Thank you for contacting ABC Company". If someone has replied to one of your emails, be sure to say, "Thank you for your prompt reply" or "Thanks for getting back to me". Thanking the reader puts him or her at ease, and it will make you appear more polite.

State your purpose

If you are starting the email communication, it may be impossible to include a line of thanks. Instead, begin by stating your purpose. For example, "I am writing to enquire about …" or "I am writing in reference to …".

Make your purpose clear early on in the email, and then move into the main text of your email. Remember, people want to read emails quickly, so keep your sentences short and clear. You'll also need to pay careful attention to grammar, spelling and punctuation so that you present a professional image of yourself and your company.

Add your closing remarks

Before you end your email, it's polite to thank your reader one more time and add some polite closing remarks. You might start with "Thank you for your patience and cooperation" or "Thank you for your consideration" and then follow up with, "If you have any questions or concerns, don't hesitate to let me know" and "I look forward to hearing from you".

End with a closing

The last step is to include an appropriate closing with your name. "Best regards", "Sincerely", and "Thank you" are all professional. Avoid closings such as "Best wishes" or "Cheers" unless you are good friends with the reader. Finally, before you hit the send button, review and spell check your email one more time to make sure it's truly perfect!

EMAIL MARKETING

Staying competitive is very important in any business environment and this is more so relevant when applied to the world of internet marketing. Using the email marketing tool is a good start in the right direction. This style of direct marketing a message is both quick and effective when comparisons are made with other available platforms. Get the info here.

Reaching the target audience with email marketing strategies will provide several positive and beneficial liaisons. Some of these include enhancing the relationships of the merchant and customer pools, encouraging the customer loyalty and thereby effectively ensuring repeat business.

There is also the avenue to pursuing new customers this way as it creates the circumstances to reach the said customer base for the purpose of encouraging an immediate purchase.

Providing the customer base with complimenting information from other affiliates is also beneficial for the customer.

Through the email marketing strategies, information taking the form of email newsletters can be both informative and relationship building as the customer will be kept well informed while at the same time addressing the customers' needs.

Transactional emails are also helpful in providing the means for the customer to respond accordingly to the merchant, such as dropped basket messages, purchases, order confirmations and many more.

The direct emails are mainly used for the purpose of informing customers of current promotions, announcements, momentary special services available among others.

Most individuals using this tool have found it to be very helpful in tracking the returns on investments and its often only second best to search marketing.

Being able to reach a wider audience base is also another positive attribute of this emailing tool. Countering these, are also disadvantages which contribute to the ineffectiveness of the whole process. This includes the ability of the customers being able to block mails and also the possibility of contravening spam laws.

Having a substantial email list is very important to the success of any internet business venture. This is more so because most of the customer base begins through this portal. There all measures should be taken to ensure the subscribers list is long and beneficial to both parties.

Sign Ups

There are a few points that should be considered in the quest to garner as many subscribers as possible. Some of which are as follows:

Designing the forms, responses and other interactive tools to be as visible as possible and easily accessible is very important. Providing incentive for potential signups will encourage the viewer to be more inclined to do so. Also providing interesting links that the viewer may find useful will eventually lead to the viewer signing up to gain access

Being constantly aware of what is being offered and how it's being offered will also allow the host to stay abreast and relevant which in turn will attract more subscribers. Material posted should be kept updated periodically as potential subscribers will be drawn to the site more often if this feature is diligently monitored.

In order to be able to constantly attract the attention needed to ensure a good percentage of subscribers there are several complimenting tools that can be used such as through blogs, forum postings, other lists, networking and many more.

The blogs should provide good and interesting information which should include some form of participation from the viewer to encourage a sign-up.

Forum posting are also another platform to explore as those who visit such sites already have a pre existing interest in the subject matter.

Therefore including links that direct them back to one's site will be advantages in converting them into subscribers. Forwarded emails are also an excellent source of garnering potential subscribers as it gives a glimpse into the individual's site.

Most people become tagged as unsubscribers because of the initial bombardment of emails that cause them to be unresponsive.

This unresponsiveness can be due to a variety of reasons but the most common one would be simply being fed up with unwanted solicitation or thinly veiled sales pitches. Therefore in order to limit the situation one should be weary of causing potential respondents from being unresponsive.

Get Them To Stay

Here are some ways to adopt to limit the unsubscribes:

Keep all emails on the topic promised. If there is a need to insert other material keeping it brief would be prudent. The visitor is probably only visiting the site for specific reasons and does not want to be deluged with other non related issues.

Using the personalized address system in the auto responder will create the illusion of making the individual feel special and respected. The use of names is a good tool to exploit and cannot be overdone or over emphasized.

Limiting the amount of emails sent in a week to about two or three would be ideal. Too many emails with the same content would not only become a nuisance to the receiver but the information would be redundant too. Too many emails will overwhelm the receiver and thus eventually cause them to be unresponsive. Allowing the customers to choose the frequency of emails sent to them will also encourage better relationships. The customer perceives the sender to be professional and committed.

Avoid hard selling at the onset of the email exchange. Directing the subscriber to the website where an informative and in-depth presentation can be viewed will allow the viewer to feel more comfortable and convinced to sign on.

The website material should be designed to sufficiently "sell" the featured items. However it should be noted that keeping a longer period between emails sent is also not encouraged as the idea is to keep the website relevant to the subscriber.

Using Transactional Emails

Emails are ideally supposed to keep the relationship between sender and receiver fresh and relevant al all times. Therefore care should be taken not to embellish this rather delicate relationship.

The Balance

In order to use transactional emails to its optimum benefit, some of the following points should be considered:

Personalized greeting is always a sure winner. Generally people are happy to be considered special thus addressing the emails accordingly, successfully gives this impression.

This is especially so when the element of exchange of money and goods are involved.

Including as much detail as possible without being too boring is also another feature that should be noted in the transactional email style. Callously thanking the sender for a positive response will not be sufficient. Depicting the details will ensure both parties are in agreement with what is to transpire and it also helps to avoid future misunderstandings and problems.

Always ensure the customer support contact details are clearly displayed such as toll free phone numbers, mailing addresses, links to online contacts and any other relevant information the customer may need.

There is nothing more frustrating for the customer when such information is not forth coming.

The transactional emails should also include a link to the home page easily, as there maybe a variety of reasons the customer may need to make some reference to the original material available only on the home page.

Some find it useful to also include other feature like email newsletters and special promotions and offers. Also popularly included are RSS feeds for updated information and products. Loyalty programs, customer forums, blogs, social-network sites are also recommended to be included for added advantage.

Sometimes there is a need to include guidelines on the item's use and makeup which is helpful to the receiving party. This will help to cut down the time spent trying to decipher the product's functions.

Using Triggers In The Email

Perhaps understanding what this tool is first before deciding to use it should be explored for obvious benefits. Simply explained, triggers are pieces of SQL which causes activation when certain events or actions occur. When new data is inserted into a program the user is able stay abreast with these new developments through the triggers as and when they are activated.

Triggers

These triggers are very useful when compared to the task of having to individually alert subscribers to new materials available. An ideal trigger template should include the following items like creating the trigger (new menu) SQL, using specific value for template parameters, commands (Ctrl-Shift-M) which fill the parameter and other more technical needs.

Triggers in emails allow the time frame for the marketing pitch to be suited to the customer's needs without having to assert too much effort.

This trigger based platform is both effective and precise in assisting the marketing programs to seize the moments and make an impact.

This provides the hosting party to be able to entice the customer at just the right time with just the right amount of knowledge so as not to be perceived as pushy and thus off putting.

Not requiring any constant monitoring is also another reason for the popularity of the trigger tool. These triggers are ideals as complimenting partners to broader programs like newsletters, special offers and acquisition programs.

This is made more attractive because it is primarily activated through customer behavioural patterns. Because the customer initiating action is the focal point of the triggers the responses are also more likely to be favourable. It has been noted that the results have been encouraging and customer satisfaction rates have improved.

There has been a documented improvement in response rates when compared to the more conventional emailing campaigns. This of course is good news to those concerned about bombarding their emailing listed customers into submission.

Testing Different Variations Of Your Email

Already noted is the fact that email campaigns are for most the focal point of the business harnessing tools. Therefore it is interesting and exciting to note that this particular tool can be changed constantly until desired results are met. Testing the many variations possible for the email format design can be quite a challenge but none the less a rewarding one.

Check It Out

Below are just some of the areas where the variable theory can be applied:

Starting from the basics would be the exercise of finding the best suited and result proven sender information. Finding the suitable name, company name, keyword or any other addressing term that denotes branding building and recognition is important.

When this is successfully identified it should be kept and used consistently and without further change unless deemed necessary and beneficial.

The subject line also has to be measured for its opening rate until the most suitable combination is found.

The same concept should be applied to the measurement of the click rate and conversion rate for the content element. These should include the different variances for personalization, wording, call to action, layout, numbers, placements, images, lengths and many other connective content matters.

Gauging the opening rates based on the times of a day is also another variant that can and should be tried out.

In identifying the "peak" opening times the host will be better positioned for business.

Varying the landing pages content to suit the needs of the possible masses is also recommended. Designing the landing pages to be attractive enough to encourage further interest is vital to getting click converted to committed customers.

Ultimately the idea should be to keep the customer engaged within the initial click on the landing page without too many complicated follow up steps.

Use Analytics To Separate Buyers From Non Buyers

The success of online businesses depends largely on the exposure rate and impact the website makes on the visitor. This is very important to the first impression being formed as the merchant does not have the luxury of personal contact to gauge the customer's wants and needs of the time. Therefore tools like information derived from analysis would have a rather profound impact on the online business success rate.

Gauge It

Some of the items that should be considered when creating a conducive platform to encourage transactions would be to know some basic information on the demographics intended.

This information should cover geographical locations, family make-up, buying power and it should help to identify the target buyer.

Serious buyers would essentially be looking into important elements like measurable quantitative terms, substantial availability of items, accessible distribution methods, sensitive and well planned affordable marketing exposure that generates the right kind of interest.

Well designed internet tools will help to detect the interest rates as their frequency and active purchases are logged. Buyer will also generally stay loyal if and when the products sought are able to maintain the promised quality and quantity without doubt.

Non buyers however will only be interested in browsing for the cheapest deals and may not necessarily make a purchase in the end.

Serious buyers also tend to be more active in surfing for the most compatible and innovative items available. These individual will stay focus and true to the intention of making a purchase thus taking the trouble to source the relevant information where and when needed.

There are several tools already available to be utilized when there is a need to track such behavioural patterns to ensure the right target audience is being reached. All this is based mostly on addressing the niche marketing sector.

Use Loyalty Programs

Having a good and strong customer base is very important to the success of any business venture. Therefore it is important to ensure the customer base stays as loyal as possible as this in turn helps to create some form of stability for the merchant.

Keep Them Coming Back

Perhaps the among the most effective ways of creating and maintaining the customer loyalty ratios lies in the ability to provide as many incentives as possible through the setting up of various loyalty programs.

These loyalty programs should ideally be able to increase the customer's interest in staying with the product over a long period of time, thus repeat purchases become a norm.
The loyalty programs should ideally give the customer the satisfaction of knowing the merchant is interested in creating an environment where the customer is encouraged to be a major part of the business. This inclusion makes the customer feel important and considered and it also inspires the customer to stay loyal as the rewards for past purchases are tagged to the next purchase.

The loyalty programs are usually designed according to information that may include information on buying patterns and preferences of the customers.

Buy ahead discounts, purchase level rewards, rebates based on spending levels, upgrades or special added benefits are all different incentives that can be included in the loyalty program to make it as enticing as possible.

The buy ahead discounts are designed to ensure the customer is locked in from the very beginning when a purchase is made. This may be done in the form of a loyalty card that entitles the purchaser to enjoy immediate discounts or free gifts with future purchases.

The other popular loyalty program item is the rebates on spending levels where the purchaser is given bigger discounts when the purchase amount passes the relevant levels.

Determine The Correct Frequency To Send Emails

The question of frequency is always as issue and here are some tips to assist in making a more informed decision.

Important Decision

Testing is one good way to start. Besides observing market trends and available information on the subject, there is a need to conduct a series of test of the various frequency rates before a suitable one is found.

Feedback is an important and valuable assisting tool to provide the information that can help make decisions which affect the business.

Soliciting feedback is usually not easy as most people would rather not take the time to respond to this but if persistent there will eventually be a response that can provide valuable information like if the material featured is too boring and lack helpful information or if the frequency of receiving the mail is perceived to be annoying or if the content is totally irrelevant or of no interest to the recipient.

If market conditions or seasonal shopping is the prime factor in the particular business being touted then some thought should be given to whether the recipient's needs are being properly addressed in the material sent.

There is a fine line between sending too much too quickly and sending too little and too infrequently for this particular niche. How experience can and usually does play a pivotal role in deciding contents and frequency.

Giving the receiving party a chance to participate in the decision on the frequency of the emails received is also another option worth exploring.

Most recipients will be happy to oblige with such information and this will in turn create the interest and eagerness for both parties in sending and receiving the intended material.

Getting the business on a recognizable platform is important but doing it in a way that brings about the opposite results is detrimental to the success of the business. Emails are an important yet tricky tool and should be carefully considered before any decision is made.

The question of frequency is always as issue and here we have provided some tips to assist in making a more informed decision.

CHAPTER NINETEEN

Corporate Identity & Branding

If you ever had a parent, or close relative, who worked for a big corporation, chances are you saw your house slowly piling up with that company's goodies over the years. From caps and coffee mugs, to notepads, t-shirts and umbrellas, your home probably looks like a souvenir shop by now.

Well, even though company swag is just a small part of what corporate identity really is, it certainly represents the most obvious and simple way of conveying a brand.

Corporate identity actually refers to the overall image of a corporation/ startup/ business in the minds of its audiences: customers, its own employees, partners, competition, etc.

Why is it important?

One reason: Your company needs to be recognizable and stand out from the rest. Corporate identity allows your brand to speak with a unique and consistent voice. In time, you begin to grow in people's minds and you start creating a particular impression in them. In a world completely flooded by advertising, this is extremely important!

For example: You are not a store that sells computers; you are Apple, whose stores are unlike any other stores; your products are sold in uniquely white boxes; your new product announcements are done in a specific format and speech style; your website resembles both your physical store and your speech from your product announcement conferences.

See where am I going here?

You need to be YOU, and people need to relate to YOU when they see you. And that goes for every single thing your company does, internally and externally, as if your product/ service/ business were a living thing.

"Corporate identity allows your brand to speak with a unique and consistent voice.

To properly establish the visual persona of your brand, companies turn to designers who specialize in creating what's called Corporate Identity Manuals (CIM). This is literally a document containing all the guidelines regarding your company's design and visual framework. They can be quite extensive, and as detailed as to specifying the margins required for the use of the logo.

Overall, here are (roughly) the 4 basic elements of a CIM:

Logotype: Bit obvious right? It's one of the most iconic things about your brand. Unfortunately, it's hard to allocate specific meanings/ emotions to logos, so growing into people's minds (and hearts) usually requires time and a solid experience to back it up.

Color Palette: There's no such a thing as "colour red" (at least not for a designer) the colour spectrum is made up of infinite colour shades, and therefore each of your colours need to be coded to be replicated over time and media. Colour is a powerful tool, so it's crucial that you are consistent in its use. The Blue Hues signify trust and alot of investment banks and equity firms use these colours.

out there, and is universally recognizable.

Typography: A font can be so iconic that some brands actually rely on them as their sole logo. Coca-Cola, FedEx, CNN and Ray-Ban are just some of them. This is why typography is a great way of achieving distinction.

Imagery: Are the images full-body shots? Are they close-ups of hands? Are they landscape photos? Are they heavily contrasted? Are they color filtered? Images have a style, same as text and colors, and so they should be chosen according to a specific set of guidelines.

If you're starting your own company, or your business is rather small, you may think it's not the time to create an Identity Manual just yet. You might want to think again. Companies on the rise are among the ones who can benefit the most out of adopting a visual identity early on. It gives credibility and a sense of establishment beyond one's belief, specially in the eyes of your customers. If you don't have the resources to hire someone, at least use the elements we just showed you and try to have some consistency across your various outputs.

How to translate Corporate Identity into your slides?

Now that we know the basic elements of Visual Identity, let's see how they can be translated into your slides!

A good way of keeping your brand on top of mind when you are presenting is to have your logo appear in your slides. Keep it subtle and discreet, along the border of the slide, but let it escort you along when you are giving your speech. If you are pitching your startup for the first time, it's very likely people will forget its name the minute you pass the first slide, so make it easy for them to remember it!

Whatever colours you choose for your business, those should be used to create your presentation. Tools like Slidebean let you easily create custom colour palettes using specific colour codes. Just keep in mind colour contrast: two colours of the same palette may not go well in a text + background combination. For more information on color choosing for presentations, check out this article.

Avoid default fonts at all costs. Since everybody uses them, it belongs to nobody in particular, and it represents no specific brand. Besides, it speaks poorly of the time you invested in designing your deck. A slight change in your typography can go a long way.

This is closely related to the tone of your Corporate Communication + Corporate Behaviour. Is the tone of your communications funny? informal? solemn? loud? Images should reflect this. Also, for the sake of a better world, avoid stock photos of people at a meeting room, posing towards the camera, nor any clip art of characters solving a puzzle, or the absolute worse: two guys in a suit shaking hands. Not only does it look absolutely hideous, but no one can relate to those images. They are super fake and make you look like an amateur.

CHAPTER TWENTY

Company Formation

Company formation is the process of registering a business as a limited company at Companies House. As a result, the business becomes a distinct legal entity. The process is also referred to as 'company incorporation' and 'company registration'.

When you incorporate a limited company, it becomes an individual 'person' in the eyes of the law. Incorporated businesses are completely separate from their owners in terms of finances, liabilities, contractual agreements, and ownership of property and assets.

The law does not view unincorporated businesses like sole traders as distinct legal entities. Therefore, there is no separation between a sole trader business and its owner in terms of finances, assets and liabilities.

Why would I register a limited company?

Generally, the main reason to register a limited company is to reduce the financial responsibility of the people who own the business. This protection is known as 'limited liability'. Private companies can be limited by shares or limited by guarantee.

The owners of a company limited by shares are only liable for the value of their shares. The owners of a company limited by guarantee are only liable for the value of their guarantees. Their personal finances and assets are protected beyond the limit of their liabilities.

This is not the case for unincorporated business structures. Sole traders, for example, are wholly liable for all business debts and liabilities because there is no legal or financial distinction between the individual person and the business.

Aside from the obvious benefits of personal financial protection, limited company formation creates a professional corporate image and allows business owners to manage their personal remuneration in a more tax-efficient manner.

Furthermore, limited status gives the impression of an established and reliable business. As a result, incorporated businesses are more attractive to investors, lenders, clients and suppliers.
Registering as a limited company is, therefore, an effective and affordable way to further the potential of a fledgling or existing business, attract more favourable tax rates and appeal to a wider audience.

Do I have to register with Companies House?
If you are forming a Limited Company or Partnership then most definitely yes.

If you are a Sole trade then your have to inform HMRC and informing Companies House is not necessary.

Companies House is the Registrar of Companies in the UK and an Executive Agency of the Department for Business, Innovation and Skills (BIS). All UK limited companies and Limited Liability Partnerships (LLPs), as well as overseas companies with a place of business in the UK, are legally required to register with this official government agency.

The primary role and activities of Companies House are: Incorporating and dissolving limited companies.

Receiving information about all registered companies trading in the UK.

Ensuring all corporate information on past and present incorporated businesses is available to the public.

The Companies Act 2006 governs all UK companies under a single law regime, but Companies House operates in three separate jurisdictions, each of which is served by a different registrar: England and Wales (Cardiff registrar), Scotland (Edinburgh registrar), and Northern Ireland (Belfast registrar).

A company can be registered in any one of these jurisdictions but it can operate in all parts of the UK and overseas. The registrar with whom a company incorporates simply dictates the location of its registered office address (official HQ address).

What does the company formation process involve?

Company formation is incredibly simple: only one person is required; the entire process is carried out online; applications are delivered electronically to Companies House; and approval is normally granted within 3 hours. To register a private company limited by shares or guarantee, you will require:

*Unique company name.

*Registered office address in England and Wales, Scotland or Northern Ireland.*Minimum of one director (manager).

*Minimum of one shareholder or guarantor (owner) – can also be the director.

*Memorandum and articles of association (governing documents).

*Share capital of at least one issued share (limited by shares companies only).

*Up to four Standard Industrial Classification (SIC) codes to describe what the business does.

Rapid Formations offers a wide range of online company formation packages for registering a limited company or LLP in England and Wales, Scotland or Northern Ireland. We also provide a number of professional company address services in London and Glasgow, including a Registered Office Service, a Service Address and a Business Address.

What happens if my company formation is rejected?

This happens from time to time. If your company formation is rejected by Companies House, it will probably be down to a small error or oversight that you can fix quickly and easily, so it's usually not a huge issue.

If you submit an online application through a company formation agent, you will be notified of any mistakes or missing information immediately. You can then address the error and resubmit your application online on the same day for no extra charge.

This is one of the many benefits of registering through a

company formation agent. It will take significantly longer to be notified of a rejected application and rectify any problems if you use Companies House incorporation services.

Main reasons for rejected company formation

The most common reasons a company formation is rejected are:

A company name is unavailable, incomplete or missing from the application.

A company name requires supporting evidence.

Supporting evidence for a company name has been incorrectly presented.

A company name contains a 'sensitive' word or expression.

Incomplete details are provided for a director or company secretary.

A residential address is flagged as being a commercial property.

Company share structure is incorrect.

There is a problem with an officer's authentication.

A company director does not meet the minimum age requirement of 16.

A director is registered as an undischarged bankrupt or a disqualified director.

A registered office address has not been included, or it is situated in the wrong country.

The statement of capital is incomplete or missing.

The articles of association has not been included.

Avoid rejection by being careful !

All of these errors can be easily avoided so it's worth taking your time during the application process. And remember to check the availability of your company name before submitting your application.

It will only take you a couple of minutes at most. If you choose to register your company through Rapid Formations, your application will be reviewed by a specialist agent before it is delivered to Companies House, thus significantly reducing the risk of being rejected.

In the unlikely event that your registration is not accepted, we will notify you immediately. You can also follow the progress of your application on our Online Admin Portal.

In most cases, errors can be fixed in a matter of minutes. Additional documents can be sent electronically to Companies House for no extra charge. All being well the second time around, your new limited company should be approved and ready-to-trade within 3-6 working hours.

What documents are required for company registration?

It depends whether you register through a company formation agent or Companies House. If you choose to set up a company online through a formation agency like Rapid Formations, you should not have to submit any paperwork or deal with any physical documentation. Our incorporation service is electronic and carried out entirely online.

If you decide to use the registration services provided by Companies House, however, you will have to compete form IN01, which is extensive, and deliver it online or by post. You may also have to submit certain documents, depending on whether you use the online or postal service.

Incorporating through a company formation agent.

By choosing to set up a company through a formation agency like Rapid Formations, you will require competing a simple online application form. The following electronic documents must be completed and submitted to Companies House:

Articles of association

This is the company's governing document. The articles of association sets out the rules about how the company should be run, the rights and responsibilities of the members and directors, how and when shares can be issued or transferred and how decisions should be made. We provide standard Model articles with all of our company formation packages. This version is suitable for most companies.

Supporting documentation for sensitive words in a company name.

Only required if your company name contains sensitive words or expressions that need to be approved by Companies House or another authorising body. This additional documentation may attached to your online application in the form of an email, digital file or scanned paper document, so there is no need to send anything by post.

You will authorise the submission of your application by creating a unique digital signature. When your company registration has been approved (usually within 3 hours), you will receive digital copies of your incorporation documents by email. Paper incorporation documents are also available.

Memorandum of association.

The memorandum is a declaration of the founding members (shareholders or guarantors) of the company. It that states their names and their agreement to form the company and become members by taking at least one share or guaranteeing a sum of money to the company.

You do not have to complete this form per se, but you must provide certain information during the registration process that Companies House will then enter on the memorandum. A copy will be provided to you after incorporation. The memorandum will also be displayed on the central public register of companies.

Incorporating with Companies House directly Companies House provides online and postal incorporation services that take between 2-10 days to process. You do not need to post any physical paperwork if you use the online service, unless you are resubmitting an application that was rejected or you are asked to send additional documentation.

To register a company by post, you will need to submit the following documents:

Form IN01 'Application to register a company'.

The memorandum of association.

The articles of association (unless you adopt Model articles in their entirety).

Supporting documents for the use of sensitive words or expressions in your company name

The postal application form can be used to register a company limited by shares or guarantee with model or altered articles. However, the online service from Companies House can only be used to set up a limited by shares company with Model articles and no sensitive words in its name.

Do I have to start trading when my company has been set up?

You can start trading through your limited company as soon as your company formation application is approved. Alternatively, you can make your company dormant if you don't want to start trading straight away.

The trading status of a limited company is considered to be active when:

It carries on any kind of trading or professional business activity.

Goods are bought or sold with a view to making a profit.

It provides services.

Income is received.

Interest is earned.

It manages investments.

Staff are employed.

It buys or rents property.

Informing HMRC

Companies House will inform HMRC when your new company is incorporated. You will then receive a letter from HMRC at your registered office. It will contain your company's Unique Taxpayer Reference. The letter will also provide information about what to do when your company starts trading.

If your company is trading, it is 'active' for Corporation Tax. You must tell HMRC that it is active within 3 months of carrying on any type of business activity. HMRC will update their computer records with the information you provide. They will tell you when you need to pay corporation tax and file a tax return.

If you have employees, you will have to register for PAYE. You must register for VAT if you think your annual turnover will be more than £85,000 (2017-18 VAT registration threshold). You can also voluntarily register for VAT if your turnover is below the threshold.

Can I bring in a business partner after company formation?

Yes, any time you like. A business partner could be a valuable addition to your limited company, particularly if you are running your business single-handedly. However, before you agree to appoint a new director or bring in new shareholders, you must be certain that your chosen sidekick has the necessary skills and knowledge to successfully manage all aspects of the business.

You must also ensure he or she supports your company's values and vision, that your personalities and attitudes can integrate well and enable you to work collaboratively, and that you maintain overall control by retaining a majority stake in the business.
The introduction of a business partner is an effective way to raise additional capital, expand your business or fund a new project, share the burden of operational responsibility and financial liability, and provide expert skills and knowledge to complement your own.

However, before you make any commitments, we strongly recommend seeking expert legal advice because it can be difficult to get rid of someone once they have a financial stake in a business. The right partner could be the making of your business, but the wrong one could prompt its swift demise.

Selling company shares to a new business partner

If you wish to bring in an equity partner (shareholder), you will require selling some of your own shares or issuing new shares in exchange for capital investment. Ideally, this is something you should take into consideration during the company formation process because your long-term plans will affect the number of shares you decide to issue.

Related: A guide to shares in a limited company

If you are likely to bring in a business partner at some point after company formation, you should issue more than one share when you register with Companies House. This will make it easier to sell some of your shares at a later date. If you issue only one share to yourself, you have no shares to give to anyone else. This is not a huge problem. You will simply have to increase the issued capital by allotting new shares in your company. However, this is more time consuming and costly than selling existing shares.

To transfer (sell) some of your own shares, you will have to complete a Stock Transfer Form. If you need to increase the issued capital and create new shares, you will have to complete a Return of Allotment of Shares and file it with Companies House within one month. If your new business partner will be appointed as a director, you must complete Form AP01 and file it with Companies House within one month.

CHAPTER TWENTY ONE

Landing Pages & Websites

In digital marketing, a landing page is a standalone web page, created specifically for the purposes of a marketing or advertising campaign. It's where a visitor "lands" when they have clicked on a Google AdWords ad or similar.

Landing pages are designed with a single focused objective – known as a Call to Action (CTA). This simplicity is what makes landing pages the best option for increasing the conversion rates of your Google AdWords campaigns.

To fully understand the difference between a landing page, and the other pages on your website, such as your homepage, it's important to consider the differences between organic search traffic and paid search traffic. Landing Pages and Organic vs. Paid Search Traffic

When asking the question, "What is a landing page?" you need to understand that they are designed for paid traffic like Google Adwords. The image opposite shows a typical Google search results page (SERP) that you might see after entering a search query.

There are four main areas:

1. Paid Search Results: Google AdWords

2. Paid Search Results: Google Shopping Ads

3. Google Featured Snippet

4.Organic Search Results

The organic search results are the links to your website that Google has chosen to show in response to the search query. This is why you have a website – to be found through organic search.

The paid search results are different. For paid advertising, you get to choose where the link takes your visitors. You could choose to send them to your websites homepage, or to the preferred option – a standalone landing page created specifically for that ad campaign.

The Difference Between a Homepage and a Landing Page

Having fewer links on your landing page has been proven to increase conversion rates when it comes to paid advertising, as there are fewer available distractions. Which is why expert marketers doing paid advertising always use a dedicated standalone landing page as the destination of their ad traffic.

Different Types of Landing Page

There are two basic structural types of landing page:

1) Lead Generation landing pages (sometimes referred to as lead gen or lead capture pages) use a web form as the Call to Action, for the purpose of collecting lead data such as names and email addresses. This is the primary type of landing page used for B2B marketing.

2) Click-Through landing pages are typically used for e-commerce and have a simple button as the Call to Action.

CHAPTER TWENTY TWO

Inspiration

List of most expensive domain names

This is a list of some of the highest prices paid for domain names. The list is limited to domains that sold for $3 million or more.

1. Insurance.com $35.6 million in 2010
2. VacationRentals.com $35 million in 2007
3. PrivateJet.com $30.18 million in 201
4. Internet.com $18 million in 2009
5. 360.com $17 million in 2015
6. Insure.com $16 million in 2009
7. Fund.com 2008 £9.99 million
8. Sex.com for $14 million in November 2014
9. Hotels.com $11 million in 2001
10. Porn.com 2007 $9.5 million
11. Porno.com for $8,888,888 in Feb 2015
12. Fb.com by Facebook for $8.5 million November 2010
13. Business.com for $7.5 million in December 1999
14. Diamond.com 2006 $7.5 million
15. Beer.com 2004 $7 million
16. iCloud.com by Apple Inc. for $6 million in March 2011
17. Israel.com for $5.88 million in May 2008
18. Casino.com 2003 $5.5 million
19. Slots.com 2010 for $5.5 millio
20. Toys.com: Toys 'R' Us by auction for $5.1 million 2009
21. AsSeenOnTv.com 2000 for $5.1 milliom
22. Clothes.com 2008 $4.9 million
23. Medicare.com 2014 $4.8 million
24. IG.com 2013 September for $4.6 million

25. Marijuana.com 2011 for $4.20 million
26. GiftCard.com by Card Lab for $4 million October 2012
27. Yp.com by YellowPages.com $3.8 million Nov 2008
28. Mi.com by Xiaomi for $3.6 million in April 2014
29. AltaVista.com for $3.3 million in August 1998
30. Whisky.com for $3.1 million in December 201
31. Vodka.com for $3.0 million in 2006
32. Candy.com for $3.0 million in June 2009
33. Loans.com by Bank of America $3.0M February 2000

CHAPTER TWENTY THREE

How to find Buyers

Domain investing involves many different techniques, ideally crafted toward your investment goals and risk tolerance.

You probably have your own niche, custom approach but how do you keep up-to-date with all the different techniques?
To aid in optimizing your own strategy, various resources on domain investing as well as tools can help your domain acquisition and investment techniques.

Set Goals to Inform a Strategy

We all want to make money at the end of the day. But having a focused approach with specific goals in mind can help direct your activities as well as indicate when you've achieved them. You have to ask yourself are you looking for a short-term (and potentially smaller) gain, or are you looking to take advantage of a trend for a potentially larger gain over a longer time period? Setting your expectations on the amount of your investment, return on investment and preparing for possible contingencies can help define your "entry" and "exit" strategy for your investment in a domain name and drive you to success.

Configure strategies into a domain purchase and investing plan

Here are some areas you can use to create a business plan:

Learn from well known investors in the industry.
Don't be afraid to contact people and ask questions. There are a number of investors who will share their experience and knowledge. Decide on a strategy, and from the knowledge others can impart about various monetization strategies can be critical in optimizing or augmenting your own approach.

Keep up with the industry and popular trends.
The internet is minefield of information, take advantage of this and read news stories, popular culture trends, and industry trends which are events that can trigger a rush in domain name purchases. To stay abreast of key events, there are a number of industry publications, feeds, tickers and other resources that can help you find and analyze relevant and timely domain names. Many tools can help you analyze a domain name's potential traffic and keyword competition, narrow on your "niche" trend and help provide functionality to notify you in real time.

Choose proven top-level domains (TLDs).
The standard way of thinking in the domain business is demonstrated that TLDs, for example, .com, ,nets ,orgs represent a general safe speculation with the most noteworthy, with a high average sale in the auxiliary market as indicated by Sedo, which portrays its domain marketplace as the most dynamic in the domain industry. Furthermore, as opposed to a few cases, there are still a lot of opportunities to put resources into, and benefit from, .com domain names.

Previously registered names can offer great value.

Sometimes the greatest finds are names that could be sources of traffic, such as previously registered domain names that have recently expired. There are tools that can help you find a domain name days before it's back on the market. Time is critical so you can register your preferred choices before others. Many of these names may have been registered by an individual, business, etc. and could have traffic although the website no longer exists. For instance, Verisign data shows that 108 million .com names that were once registered are available now. Use information and knowledge about the market to help you vet and validate these opportunities.

Trademark Domain Names.

Some strategies can prove to be costly and registering domain names containing a trademark or even a word that is close to a trademarked word, such as typosquatting, can have legal implications. As you search for domain names of significance, it is important to understand the trademark laws and the elements of trademark infringement actions and the dispute procedures in the domain name industry including the Uniform Domain-Name Dispute-Resolution Policy (UDRP) and the Uniform Rapid Suspension (URS) process. Remember, parties can file a claim against registrants who register domain names that contain trademarks or words that are close to, or confusingly similar to, trademarks.

How to become a successful domain investor today.

If you're new to the domain name buying and selling business you may want to follow me on Instagram, connect with me on LinkedIn or chat to me via my Websites.*"Domains will continue to go up in value faster than any other commodity ever known to man." quote unconfirmed but apparently has been said by two famous people.*

You can start buying domains and make a living from it today. But before you do you need to do your due diligence and get familiar with the domain name industry. Generic domains have become expensive over the years and they'll not stop going up in value anytime soon.

Therefore, you must concentrate on cheaper domains and a way of finding good but affordable domains is to be creative. Below I've compiled a list with a few tips on how to get into the domain business if you don't have enough money to buy your way into the high end of the market.

1. Register domains names

When your starting out start small and build up your portfolio. Do not go to the bank and get a loan to buy thousands of domains, that just careless.

Work slowly up and within your means, if you cannot live without the money then think again, as putting food on the table and keeping a roof over your head is more important than risking your money on domain names. Yes there is a chance your domain names may never sell, always proritise your living expenses first.

If you are confident you can manage without the money you can then test the markets and see if you flip your first lot of domains before going full blazing saddles ahead. Obviously registering a lot of domains is one method, but many new domainers have failed trying. Most of them failed because they started registering domains before they knew anything about the value of them, which meant they registered worthless domains and threw money down the drain.

The first thing to do before stuffing money into the pockets of your favorite domain registrar is to read as much about domains as you can. You will find useful advice on any of the domain forums or in books and blogs.

There is money to be made with newly registered domain extensions. You do not have to get your hands on high-value domains, but it should be domains that can be resold for a profit. What you can try to do, is to register domains at £10 each and then resell them for £20 each. Keep in mind that there Escrow fees involved or brokerage commissions. Also do not forget that the bank will want to make some money converting the money into your currency. If you resell a domain at £30 you would have made a £20 profit. This is a hypothetical example as you need to take into account and calculate all the exchange rate fee as well as the marketplace you are selling your domains on.

Although this is not much money but if you did this in volumn and set a goal of turning over a £1 Million within 5 years you would only have to sell 55 domain names a day for the next five years at a cost of £10 per domain name sold at double the price would leave you with a profit of £1,003,750.00

Your aim should be to quickly resell hundreds of domains.

After a few months of successful domain reselling you might find yourself in a financially better position to purchase domains on the aftermarket. Additionally, you've completed several domain transactions and gained hands-on experience about how to sell and transfer domain names. You can then reinvest the domain you made in higher quality domains, which are for sale on domain forums and domain marketplaces.

The question on everyone's mind is "how do I find sellable domain names"? Think like the person who is searching for something on the web use the keyword they would use,concentrate on domains that are generic in nature and are pronounable. Use Google's AdWords Keyword Tool to find popular search terms Google has most recently changed their Console you still have the option to use the old version but I would customise myself with the newer version as this is the one that is going to stay. Occasionally I also use Google Trends for seasonal search terms, but most of the time I ready in Business Magazines, Blogs and Forums.

I personally scour Business Tech news to see the latest inventions and use the keyword to find domain names. Think of the future and all the new inventions that are coming out. So be creative and think of domains that can help an end user make money, and you should be able to come up with domains worth significantly more than the fee for registration.

2. Register domains (lower volume approach)

If you don't want to start making money in domaining by reselling domains at £xx each, you can try to register or acquire fewer domains that you think will have potential in the future, e.g. domains for upcoming technologies. Such speculative domain registrations usually take longer to turn into a profit, but they have the potential to sell for higher prices should they really become valuable at some point in the future.

In order to find domains with future potential it would be a good idea to subscribe to lots of blogs and to read technology and science magazines, because you must spot trends early on.

3. Limited supply

Three-letter domains were not considered very valuable once. But as you probably know, three-letter domains only rarely sell for less than high $x,xxx today anymore. This little piece of domain history should teach you that domains can become valuable if they're limited in quantity.

Four-letter domains can still be bought for $xx to $xxx, depending on the letters they contain. Some CVCV.COM domains have also been sold for prices in the four-figure range. And a major corporation, NBC Universal, has chosen the four-letter domain hulu.com for their new YouTube rival. You see, there is value in LLLL.COM domains and now would be the time to invest.

Before venturing into accronyms I would use AcronymFinder.com to find out about the possible meanings of LLL/LLLL domains you want to buy. But you and your buyer would have to do extensive ardvertising to get the brand name established and well known. Consider these factors, before investing.

Sometimes dropped auction offer golden nuggets try Godaddy Basement Bucket to see what has been dropped. Remember you will not be able to sell these domain names straight away as they are locked by the registrars for up to 60 days.

Every day you can buy expired domains in drop auctions. You can either use Godaddy.com or SnapNames.com. Dropped domains are a good way to find proftable assets at cheap prices. Godaddy sell their dropped domains for as little as $5.00 which is about £3.00 in UK Currency. You may get lucky and find highly valuable generic domains on the daily drop lists which the previous owners mistakenly or stupidly let expire.

An expired domain service catches expired domains and auctions them off to its users. At SnapNames.com the minimum bid is usually lower than $100 per domain. This makes it a great source for valuable domains that can be bought below value, because some good domains are overlooked among the high number of names dropping every day. If you're lucky you're the only person who expressed interest in a particularly nice domain and you then get it for the minimum bid without having to go to auction.

Many expiring domains have been actively used and therefore have a history. The following tools can help you determine if an expiring domain is likely to receive traffic:Whois tools: Look up the creation date and expiration date of a domain name (e.g. iWhois.com)

5. Development

If you're good at making websites you can register or buy a few domains and develop them into useful websites or full online businesses. Developing a domain requires lots of work, but it is rewarding in the end, as you will be able to sell the domain plus website for a price much higher than what you would get for the domain name alone. In addition, developed websites can make money from Google AdSense or affiliate ads (Commision Junction or Rakuten Linkshare).

Today it's easier than ever to develop a website, because there are various open source content management systems that let you build large and interactive websites without requiring deep knowledge in PHP programming. WordPress is a popular solution, for instance. Joomla is also good if you want to launch a bigger site. Both programs make it easy to customize your website with plug-ins and downloadable templates.

If you want to develop a domain of yours, don't forget that you're developing it for "human beings". This might seem obvious, but many "developers" just put up made-for-AdSense sites with duplicate content nowadays. A domain+website will be more valuable and it will receive more traffic if it is unique and has quality content to offer.

CHAPTER TWENTY FOUR

Domain Theft & Scams

Naming and Shaming!

Finally there is a website to name and shame corporate scammers. I could think of at least one person I would love to put on this website, but unfortunately he does not fit into this criteria .

Although this one particular person did not scam me for stealing my domains indirectly he did however scam by making me build websites inclusive of two domain names for him and then did not pay me.

I could go on but he was running two photographic studios, he expected me to work in this studio working on my business whilst also helping him with the photo shoots which he never paid me a single penny for.

He did pay a partial monthly fee for the webites I managed for him on the basis as soon as work picked up he would increase the payments. He refused to sign any contracts.Then out of the blue he decided to close one of the studios down because he owed money for rent and that is when he stopped paying me for all three websites. He found out what hosting company I use and registered one of the domains to that hosting company and made me build the websites around him. I had no control over the one website at all apart from a temporary back office user name and password, whilst the other two where registered to my account so I ended up closing them down.

So I have no control over the still in existence site even though he uses it to make money from day in and day out. He must have planned this all along for me not to have control over his hosting. His day will come as Google have made changes so that all websites have to have SSL Certificates and those that don't will eventually get blocked.

On the other hand the high profile Domain Name owner and publisher of this site has focused on Domain Thieves.

The website is: http://www.hallofshame.com

Domain Scams

Scammers usually find themselves in your inbox. I received an email from a Chinese registrar wanting me to give up my rights to 'www.ukwebsitedesigners.co.uk' and 'www.ukdomainbrokers.com'.

I had two options either ignore the email or reply back. I chose to respond......hopefully I won't here from them again.

Email Scams to Coerce Domain Owners to give up their domain names or buy Chinese TLDs with the same Domain Name / Brand.

What happens is Asian scammers pressurize firms to register identical domain names in Asian Top-Level-Domains. The act is called "Slamming", and is an illegal practice to mislead companies to either give up their domain names or sell them unsolicited services and domain extensions.

Unknown third party, pressure, threats, high prices…

The practice involves sending an email, written in English and adressed to the CEO of the targeted company. The scammer contacts the owner who is usually unaware of the rules and regulations related to domain names.

They present themselves as accredited Asian registrars, mainly in China. This unknown third party notifies the owner of the domain in question that one of their clients wants to register domain names containing the trademark of the target of the scam.

So what do you do when faced with slamming?

When you receive the email, contact your registered domain name registrar.

They will confirm the action as being a scam by the Asian registrar.

If your scammer has interests in the Asian region then registrations in .ASIA and in the few local Country-Code-Top-Level-Domains (ccTLDs) were you are located (ex: .HK HongKong, .IN India, .JP Japan, .KR Korea, .SG Singapore, .TW Taiwan…) are more appropriate.

Example email of scare mongering.

Dear Sir/Madam,
We have received a request for the registration of the website **www.thegoldandsilvercompany.net** Our system shows that you are the owner of **www.thegoldandsilvercompany.com** *This can have far-reaching consequences for you in the future.*

We are therefore under the statutory obligation to contact you, in order to offer you the first right of registration. This means that we will reject the application of the third party and the website:

www.thegoldandsilvercompany.net

After agreement we will link this website to:

www.thegoldandsilvercompany.com

This means that you will have the first option on the domain name, in order to avoid possible future problems.

We are usually under the obligation to register the domain name and to protect it for a period of 10 years. The annual price for the .NET extension is £19.75 per year. This means a one-off payment of £197.50. When the link has been completed, all the Internet traffic that goes to the .NET extension, will be automatically **linked** to your current extension and website. **(So if they were being genuine they would transfer the domain name not just point it to my existing one)** *I obviously smelt a rat.* This process will take a maximum of 24 hours. This domain name will then have a worldwide reach. The third party will be rejected and can no longer use your domain name.

Important information:

You will receive a one-off invoice of £197.50, exclusive of VAT, for a term of 10 years. This contract can be cancelled at all times after the first term of one year. The paid amount for the remaining number of years will be refunded to your account. If you agree to our offer, please send an agreement by email within 48 hours after receipt of this email, stating your name, address and VAT number in a reply to this email address.

The third party will subsequently be rejected by us, and we will then complete the link. You will receive a confirmation and all the information you need by email on the same day.

With kind regards,
******

The Gold and Silver Company is a website that I am selling this was one of my earliest clangers before I realised that the shorter the domain the better it is. Hence I do not recommend more than three words maximum and this website is an expception to the rule.

This is not how you should write emails - Be Safe!

CHAPTER TWENTY FIVE

Intellectual Property Law

Domains names that are trademarked are protected by Intellectual Property Rights.

Intellectual Property refers to creations of the mind: inventions; literary and artistic works; and symbols, names and images used in commerce. Intellectual property is divided into two categories: Industrial Property Industrial Property includes patents for inventions, trademarks, industrial designs and geographical indications. Copyright Copyright covers literary works (such as novels, poems and plays), films, music, artistic works (e.g., drawings, paintings, photographs and sculptures) and architectural design. Rights related to copyright include those of performing artists in their performances, producers of phonograms in their recordings, and broadcasters in their radio and television programs.

What are intellectual property rights?

Intellectual property rights are like any other property right. They allow creators, or owners, of patents, trademarks or copyrighted works to benefit from their own work or investment in a creation. These rights are outlined in Article 27 of the Universal Declaration of Human Rights, which provides for the right to benefit from the protection of moral and material interests resulting from authorship of scientific, literary or artistic productions.

What is a trademark?

A trademark is a distinctive sign that identifies certain goods or services produced or provided by an individual or a company. Its origin dates back to ancient times when craftsmen reproduced their signatures, or "marks", on their artistic works or products of a functional or practical nature. Over the years, these marks have evolved into today's system of trademark registration and protection. The system helps consumers to identify and purchase a product or service based on whether its specific characteristics and quality – as indicated by its unique trademark – meet their needs. Buying, Selling and Transferring.UK Website Designers buy and sell keyword related domain names that do not infringe intellectual property rights and in some cases buy domains on behalf of the owners. Once a website contract has ended UK Website Designers may transfer the ownership of the domain to the client if the domain is not owned by the client at their discretion The only time it is necessary for UK Website Designers to transfer the domains to the client is when the client can prove they are the legal owner or if the website contract has ceased. If you have questions regarding ownership of domains and wish us to resolve a dispute please do not hesitate to contact us.

However if a website designer is asked to host a domain name it will be parked with the hosting company for the lifetime of the website, it does not automatically mean that the domain name if registered by the owner belongs to the web designer. If however a person or company registers a domain name that is not trademarked it will belong to the owner until sold or transferred. If a domain consists of keywords which are not trademarked it is possible to buy and sell these words and their extensions. If a person or company owns a trademark it is not advisable to buy the domain and its extensions.

TRADEMARK

When naming your business or product or service, bear in mind other people may also come up with the same name. In order to protect one self it is always a good idea to trademark your name, may it be a logo or words, product, slogan or symbol.

The definition of a trademark can mean a protected name, word, slogan, design, symbol or other unique device that identifies a product or company.

To stop someone copying your photograph or text, music etc this falls under copyright, where you have to prove you were the one that took the photograph or wrote the text.

When it comes to an idea or invention this falls under Patent Laws stopping anyone else claiming rights.

To trademark your brand you must first register it with a Governing Body and it may take anything between 6 and 18 months to be processed.

When registering your trade mark you have to consider if you want it trade marked globally. If you register in the UK you are not protecting yourself globally, you are only protecting yourself in the UK where you have applied for the trademark. The European Union, now has a Community Trade Mark (CTM) which covers the mark in all EU countries.

The same goes if you live in the UK but you do not want the USA to use your brand name you have to also register your trademark in the USA and any other subsequent countries.

To trademark you brand in bulk there is also the Madrid System that provides a facility to submit trademarks applications to many countries at the same time.

You cannot use trademark symbols without registering your brand first this is illegal to do. Registered trademarks may be signified by the abbreviation 'TM', or the '®' symbol.

You can also patent your brand but this is more for inventions rather than for trademarks although in most countries, the national patent office will in most cases also administer trademarks. But the best way to go is to contact your Government for application.

Links to all Government websites can be found here:

https://www.copyrightservice.co uk/copyright/intellectual_property

What could happen in future is that Domain Investors buy up the domains and later on find someone has trade marked the name a little later down the line, proving your domain to be worthless. But this is where you would have to argue what came first the chicken or the egg...

So your most probably reading a lot about UDRP so what are they exactly?

UDRPs is the short name for Uniform Domain Name Dispute Resolution Policy, where by you have registered or you have acquired the domain name simply for the purpose of selling, renting, to the complainant who is the owner of the trademark or service mark of a brand name for a hign value.

In other words cybersquatting.

It can happen to the best of us, but to avoid such matters do your research make sure no one else is using the name and that it does not have the letter (R) or (TM) next to it.

But as it stands this Trademarking is giving the domain industry a bad name if the legitimate domainers buy the domains in good faith only to have someone else trademark that name after they have acquired it, that to me would be unfair.

So someone buys a domain name and someone else jumps on the band wagon and goes ahead and trademarks that word. Which brings me back to what came first the chicken or the egg. I feel I'm walking on egg shells talking about this, but something needs to be done whereby the moment you buy the domain you should have full registration ownership, providing no one else has trademarked it before you.

INTELLECTUAL PROPERTY INFRINGEMENT

However this is were it gets a bit confusing if you were just buying the name say for instance www.gucci.wales then that would be illegal but if you bought up the domain www.guccishoes.com and you were a retailer or stockist of Gucci Shoes then providing you could prove you were the official retailer/stockist you could probably own that domain, it would not necessarily mean that Gucci should have rights to that domain name so that no one else could use it, because then it would be more difficult for original retailers and stockists to sell the brand.

It is always best to find out if a word or words are trade marked or not before going ahead and buying up domain and their extensions. If you think the word is a brand name stay away from it at all costs.

If on the other hand if its a generic word (s) then any Tom, Dick or Harry can own it.

Although in my case my client has a similar domain to mine so out of respect to my client who wants me to be involved in his business I may use my domain to increase the SEO for that business. God know what he is going to do with all the other extensions available on the market for the two keywords, unless he tries to buy them all.

Here is the link to the government website outlining intellectual property rights in the UK: https://www.gov.uk/guidance/intellectual-property-crime-and-infringement

If you have a problem with your domain or need some advise please email **lawdept@startbrand.co.uk** and we will pass it on to our team of solicitors.

Further reading.... here are some examples of some famous law suits.

1) S. Victor Whitmill v. Warner Bros. Entertainment Inc.
Mike Tysons tattoo artist sued Warner Bros in the film Hangver II when they used his design on Stu Price the dentist, played by Ed Helmes. The court ordered Warner Bros to change the tattoo and compensated the tatoo artist Victor Whitmill an undisclosed sum.

2) Isaac Newton v. Gottfried Wilhelm Leibniz

Isaac Newton and Gottfried Wilhelm Leibniz worked together in the early 18th century, inventing the study of calculus. Gottfried Leibniz had published his findings on the topic in 1684 and 1686. However Isaac Newton published a book called Opticks in 1704, where he claimed himself as the inventor of calculus. This caused an argument between the two.

Isaac claimed he wrote about the topic in1665 and 1666, but only told about his work with a few colleagues.

Sir Isacc Newton accused Gottfied Leibniz of plagiarizing his work. The law suit was never settled as Gottfried Leibniz died in 1716 before the case had finaized.

Today Historians claim that both Newton and Leibniz were the co-inventors, having come to the idea independently of each other, but would that have been the case when the two of them were alive?

3) Adidas America Inc. v. Payless Shoesource Inc.

Its all about the stripes, now this brings me back to the Gucci example earlier where a retailer could buy up the name www.guccishoes.com but in theory sell similar look a like shoes, this would them be illegal. The domain I am referring to is just an example and checking it today I find it is being re-directed to a website http://www.viralsharebuzz.com which has nothing to do with shoes. What I think 'Viral Share Buzz' are doing is using www.guccishoes.com to generate traffic for themselves.

If I were Gucci I would not allow anyone to use the name in any context as the name is trade marked.

Going back to Adidas.........

In 1994, Adidas and Payless got into an argument over stripes. The famous brand name and logo of the three stripes was infringed by another company using two and four stripes. Adidas had used its three-stripe mark as a logo from 1952, and had only recently registered it as a trademark. However Payless was selling athletic training shoes with two and four parallel stripes supposedly confusing the buyers market.

Remember Addidas is a trade mark of three stripes. So their argument was that no one else can have two stripes, four stripes or five etc?

However any person who is willing to spend money would know the difference between the originals and the lookalikes.

If it was simple counterfeiting then I would understand Addidas having some sort of say in the matter or if the shoe looked the same as the counterparts with one stripe less or one stripe more and the words Adidas on shoe or Didasi plastered over the shoe, then yes there could be a case.

The two companies eventually agreed out a settlement. However after the settlement Payless continued selling the look-alikes.

Adidas worried that the trainers would confuse buyers and tarnish Adidas's name, Adidas America Inc. demanded a jury re-trial.

The trial went on for seven years, during which 268 pairs of Payless shoes were examined. Adidas was awarded $305 million—$100 million for each stripe and the trial was published in the Wall Street Journal's Law Blog.

So anyone thinking of going into business should also have an original logo and register it. If Payless had trademarked their two stripe version that looked nothing like Adidas collections, they would have saved themselves $305 million.

Trademarking is not as expensive as some may think.
Go to the UK Governement website: https://www.gov.uk/how-to-register-a-trade-mark/apply

CHAPTER TWENTY SIX

UDRP & URS

What is UDRP & URS

Uniform Domain-Name Dispute-Resolution Policy

(UDRP)

General Information

Registrars are obliged to follow the Uniform Domain-Name Dispute-Resolution Policy (usually referred to as the "UDRP") Where there is a trademark dispute in which a company comes forward to make a complaint that a domain name has been registered under false pretences. Under the policy, most types of trademark-based domain-name disputes must be resolved by agreement, court action, or arbitration before a registrar will cancel, suspend, or transfer a domain name. Alleged disputes that arise from abusive registrations of domain names (for example, cybersquatting) may be addressed by expedited administrative proceedings that the holder of trademark rights initiates by filing a complaint with an approved dispute-resolution service provider.

To start proceedings and expedite the policy, a trademark owner should either (a) file a complaint in a court of proper jurisdiction against the domain-name holder (or where appropriate an in-rem action concerning the domain name)

or (b)

in cases of abusive registration submit an official complaint to an approved dispute-resolution service provider such as an ICANN approved attorney or solicitor specializing in UDRPs.

What is the Uniform Rapid Suspension System (URS)?

A trademark owner can file a complaint for the dispute of a domain name. The Uniform Rapid Suspension System (URS) is a domain name dispute policy and if successful the trademark owner can get a domain name temporarily taken offline. Like the long standing Uniform Domain Name Dispute Resolution Policy (UDRP), the URS is an effective way to combat cybersquatting against their trademark brands).

URS was created a speedy and less cost effective method to resolve a domain name dispute. However, unlike the UDRP, the URS largely applies only to the "new" generic top-level domains (that is, those approved following ICANN's 2012 domain name expansion process) – not to .com, .net, .org and the other traditional top-level domains. And, also unlike the UDRP, which allows a trademark owner to get a domain name transferred to itself, the URS only provides for a temporary measure of the problematic domain name.

The URS's Three-Part Legal Test

The legal compliance test for a URS complaint is almost the same as for a UDRP complaint. Usually, the URS requires a trademark owner, or "complainant," to show all three of the following:

1) The disputed domain name is the same as or misinterpreted word mark that meets a certain criteria.

2) The domain name registrant of the said domain name, or the "respondent," has no legitimate right or interest to the domain name.

3) The domain name was falsely registered on the pretence of being used fraudulently.

The main difference between this three-part examination and the three-part test under the UDRP is that the first part under the UDRP applies to **any** mark in which the complainant has rights (including marks that are protected by common law or marks that are not word marks). The URS, though, only applies to a word mark "(i) for which the Complainant holds a valid national or regional registration and that is in current use; or (ii) that has been validated through court proceedings; or (iii) that is specifically protected by a statute or treaty in effect at the time the URS complaint is filed."

The trademark owner must prove without a shadow of doubt on all three of these counts to succeed in a URS proceeding. In other words, even if a complainant fails on only one citing, the arbitrator is required to issue a decision in favour of the respondent, allowing the registrant to keep the disputed domain name.

Not only must the trademark owner prove without probable cause on all three parts of the URS legal examination, but it also must meet a very high clear cut and precise evidence as the URS itself specifies. URS verifies that this arbitration process is "not intended for use in any proceedings with open questions of fact, but only clear cases of trademark abuse."

This is certainly a more difficult type of proceeding than the "preponderance of evidence" standard that has emerged from UDRP doctrine.

URS Dispute Providers

A URS complaint can be filed at any ICANN-approved legal firm – currently, the Forum (formerly the National Arbitration Forum) or the Asian Domain Name Dispute Resolution Centre (ADNDRC). Although the Forum is based in Minneapolis (USA) and the ADNDRC has multiple locations in Asia, all URS filings are conducted online.

The World Intellectual Property Organization (WIPO), which is the largest UDRP service provider, does not offer URS services. Similarly, the Czech Arbitration Court accepts UDRP but not URS filings.

The URS filing fees are significantly less costly than the UDRP filing fees charged by the largest providers. The Forum's fees begin at US $375 (for complaints that include up to 14 disputed domain names), and the ADNDRC's fees start at $360 (for up to five domain names). Respondents must pay a fee for proceedings that include 15 or more domain names (though the response fee is refundable to the prevailing party), and additional fees are charged for re-examinations, re-examination extensions and appeals – all of which are options not available under the UDRP.

Mechanics and Timeline for URS Proceedings

A URS complaint is filed online, and the requirements are much more stringent than for UDRP proceedings. Among other things, for example, a complaint is limited to 500 words (as opposed to 5,000 words in a WIPO UDRP filing), and the number of annexes is restricted. Complaints cannot be amended, and supplemental filings are not permitted.

All URS proceedings are conducted in English (unlike UDRP proceedings, which are typically conducted, with some exceptions, in the language of the registrar's registration agreement).

A domain name registrant has 14 days to respond to a URS complaint, although an extension of up to seven additional days may be granted "if there is a good faith basis for doing so." Unlike the complaint, a response can be up to 2,500 words.

Whether the domain name registrant has submitted a response, the case file is submitted to an examiner (URS proceedings are limited to a single arbitrator, while the UDRP allows either party to elect one or three arbitrators). The examiner's determination (the URS equivalent of a UDRP decision) is due within five days after a response is filed.

If the examiner's decision is in favour of the complainant, then the registry operator is required to suspend the disputed domain name. Specifically, the URS states:

The Registry Operator shall cause the name-servers to redirect to an informational web page provided by the URS Provider about the URS. The URS Provider shall not be allowed to offer any other services on such page, nor shall it directly or indirectly use the web page for advertising purposes (either for itself or any other third party). The Whois for the domain name shall continue to display all of the information of the original Registrant except for the redirection of the name-servers. In addition, the Registry Operator shall cause the Whois to reflect that the domain name will not be able to be transferred, deleted or modified for the life of the registration.

The suspension remains in effect until the domain name is due to expire, unless the winning complainant elects to pay for one additional year of suspension "at commercial rates."

If the examiner's decision is in favour of the respondent, then "full control" of the domain name is returned to the registrant.

Re-examinations and Appeals Under the URS

Unlike the UDRP, an arbitrator's decision is not necessarily the end of the proceeding. A losing registrant that failed to submit a response (in what is then called a "default" proceeding) may "seek relief from Default via de novo review" for up to six months after the date of notice of the default and is even entitled to an additional six-month extension (that is, for a total of one year) if requested during the initial six-month extension period.

Further, either losing party – that is, the complainant or the respondent – may file an appeal (for an additional fee) within 14 days after a determination has been issued. Appeals are based on the existing record.

In addition, the URS makes clear that a determination "shall not preclude any other remedies available to the appellant, such as UDRP (if appellant is the Complainant), or other remedies as may be available in a court of competent jurisdiction."

Consequences for Losing Complainants

A complainant that loses a URS proceeding does not necessarily face any adverse consequences, although the URS includes "penalties for abuse of the process by trademark holders." Specifically, the URS states that a complaint may be deemed **abusive** if the examiner determines that:

it was presented solely for improper purpose such as to harass, cause unnecessary delay, or needlessly increase the cost of doing business; and (i) the claims or other assertions were not warranted by any existing law or the URS standards; or (ii) the factual contentions lacked any evidentiality support.

If a complainant is found to have filed two abusive complaints, then the complainant will be barred from utilizing the URS for one year.

The URS also includes penalties for a complainant that submits a **"deliberate material falsehood,"** which is defined as "an assertion of fact, which at the time it was made, was made with the knowledge that it was false and which, if true, would have an impact on the outcome on the URS proceeding".

A complainant will be barred from using the URS for one year upon the first finding of a deliberate material falsehood, and permanently upon two such findings.

Pros and Cons of the URS

The URS is clearly a less expensive and quicker process than the UDRP. For a trademark owner facing a particularly troublesome domain name, the URS may be a wise choice, even if it is only used to get a domain name rapidly suspended and later, perhaps, transferred by following up with a UDRP complaint.

However, as I've written before, the URS is not (yet, at least) proving to be a very popular dispute policy.

The URS's limited remedy – temporary suspension – is probably the leading reason why it is not being utilized more frequently. Because a suspended domain name is ultimately released to the general public, it may fall into the hands of another cybersquatter after the suspension period expires, at which point the trademark owner will have to decide whether to file yet another URS complaint (seeking only another temporary remedy via suspension) or a UDRP complaint (seeking a permanent remedy via transfer).

But the remedy is not the only drawback of the URS.

Because of the dispute policy's very high burden of proof and strict limitations on the arguments that can be included in a complaint, it is more difficult for a trademark owner to prevail in a URS proceeding than under the UDRP.

The doctrine of "passive holding" (which allows a trademark owner to win a UDRP case under certain circumstances involving a domain name that is not actively being used) appears to be less applicable to URS cases. And, URS cases involving pay-per-click (PPC) advertising sites and domain names that contain non-fanciful trademarks also pose challenges for complainants.

Ultimately, a trademark owner should consider both the URS and the UDRP before deciding how (and whether) to proceed against a cybersquatter, keeping in mind the financial, timing and remedy differences between the two dispute policies.

CHAPTER TWENTY SEVEN

The Law & Taxation of Digital Products

Buying and Selling to Countries outside of your GEO Location.

In the UK if you sell to a country in the EU you have to be **VAT Moss Registered** or pay the country directly Vat on your Digital products this includes Domain Names and E-Books.

My Recommendations.

My recommendation and advice is to set up a landing page and choose a niche that is relevant to you domains, that way you can advertise a few domains from your one category saving you time and money.

I would also recommend not using a done for you free template as all it does is show a nice destination page but without seo your domain will just float in cyberspace and will not be found unless someone types in your domain name.

Therefore it may be an idea to set up a professional website and start a blog. By doing so your landing page will get ranked quicker and you will have more chances of finding an investor, you can even refer back to your website/blog with a quick reference link rather than listing your whole portfolio.

Do not use autoblogs they just scramble old news/information to make it look like new its like using www.spinbot.com to re-write content.

Users prefer to read fresh new original content and if it serves no purpose and will not be ranked well if at all.

I read on a popular Facebook domain group that a famous domain broker which shall remain nameless was offering autoblogs for $35. What was not included was SEO. So unless you know a thing or two about Marketing and SEO and are contemplating using the auto software this is certainly not for you and the add on to the wordpress blog costs a subscription per month which he omitted to divulge.

www.startbrand.co.uk do offer a **Website Design** and a **Blog with SEO and Marketing plus Google Analytic's and a Facebook Page, Logo Design all inclusive for £49.99** per annum which equates to **$70.00** but you get more for your money using www.startbrand.co.uk It is slightly more than what the Domain Broker was offering on the Facebook Group but it is more value for money as you do not need to update your site and blog as we will do it for you, giving you more time to concentrate on your business and we use humans not bots.

Don't get me wrong this is a blog that you are reading now and it is not fancy like a wordpress blog which you can design and make it look like a professional website.

I chose for this purpose to have a quick and simple html version, it serves my purpose and I am on the first page of Google for the keywords 'UK Domain Brokers', which makes me happy and I was ranked within 3 months.

It normally takes about 12 to 18 months to get ranked for the First Page of Google providing you have done your

SEO properly. I have a few other tricks up my sleeve I use but they are trade secrets, as I do not want my Website Designing Competitors to know, if you see what I mean? Yet I will use my knowledge to optimize all my clients websites and blogs to their best advantage.

CHAPTER TWENTY EIGHT

ACCOUNTING

Digital Property Tax VAT MOSS MINI ONESTOP SHOP (VAT MOSS)

The VAT rules if you supply digital services to private consumers.

Did you know that if you sell e-books or domain names from within the UK to non business individuals you have to be VAT Moss Registered and if you sell to countries internationally you have to pay taxes in the location of the transaction. Do check your country rules and regulations on the Government websites. If one country has these regulations then most countries follow suit.

The place of taxation depends on the location of the consumer.

Where you supply digital services on a business-to consumer basis, you're responsible for accounting for VAT on the supply: to the tax authority at the VAT rate that applies in the consumer's EU member state. (This applies for UK Businesses).

The rules create a level playing field for UK businesses by removing the current competitive advantage of EU member states with lower rates of VAT.

If you're VAT-registered in the UK
You'll need to register for one of the following:
The VAT Mini One Stop Shop (VAT MOSS) VAT in the member states where you have non-business customers. If you are not VAT-registered in the UK you will need to do one of the following:

Voluntarily register for VAT in the UK under the special scheme for digital businesses and then register for VAT MOSS - your UK sales will not be liable, unless they're above the UK VAT registration threshold.

Register for VAT in the member states where you have non-business customers. Businesses outside the EU (for example, the USA) that supply digital services to consumers in one or more EU member state are also affected by the changes.

They'll either have to register for VAT MOSS in a member state, or register in each member state where they have non-business customers.

How to determine the place of supply and taxation Normal place of supply rules

For VAT purposes the place of supply rules set a common framework for deciding in which country a transaction should be subject to tax.

The rules for supplies of digital services to non-business consumers is a specific rule. You should check:

Whether it's a digital service because if it is not the general place of supply of services rules will apply the status of your customer, that is whether they're business or non-business the place of supply (that is, the member state) whether the supply must be taxed at the member state's standard or reduced VAT rate, or whether the supply is eligible for any VAT exemptions (for example, most member states exempt betting and gaming)

You need to identify the place where your consumer is based, has their permanent address, or usually resides. This will be the member state where VAT on the digital services supply is due. For example, a UK citizen is an expatiate, who works or lives most of their time in Spain, then you, as the person supplying digital services to that consumer, should charge Spanish VAT on those services and not UK VAT.

Defining digital services

Radio and television broadcasting services

These include:

*The supply of audio and audio-visual content for simultaneous listening or viewing by the general public on the basis of a programme schedule by a person that has editorial responsibility live streaming through the internet if broadcast at the same time as transmission by radio or television.

How to determine whether the customer is in business (a taxable person)or is a private consumer.

If you supply digital services and your customer does not give you a VAT registration number (VRN) then you should treat it as a business-to-consumer supply and charge the VAT due in the customer's member state.

If a customer cannot supply a VRN but claims they're in business but not VAT-registered because, for example, they're below their member state's VAT registration threshold, you can accept other evidence of your customer's business status, for example, a link to the customer's business website or other commercial documents.

It's your decision whether to accept alternative evidence that the customer is in business and your customer cannot ask you to treat a supply as business-to-business if they have not given a valid VRN.

If you accept that your customer is in business, the supply does not come within the scope of these business-to-consumer arrangements. With a cross-border business-to-business supply the customer will be responsible for accounting for any VAT due to the tax authorities in their member state.

You must complete and submit a quarterly European Community Sales List Declaration to HMRC. This allows other EU member state tax authorities to ask for details from the database where these declarations are securely stored, for taxpayer compliance and audit purposes.

Further information can be found via this link:

https://www.gov.uk/guidance/the-vat-rules-if-you-supply-digital-services-to-private-consumers

CHAPTER TWENTY NINE

CORPORATE IDENTITY & BRANDING

NAMING YOUR BUSINESS

So a startup decides to brand their company?

The first thing they will need to do is search if their brand name is available to buy.

In this business its on a first come first served basis. You could be lucky.

The next thing you need to do is design your brand, think of a favourite colour you wish to use and design a logo.

When choosing your name for instance buy up all the corresponding domain names so that some cybersquatter does not sit on your brand when you want to expand to different countries.

Again I read today that dot com is king. I beg to differ, just because dot com is for the american market other extensions do matter too. I personally when I buy domains buy all the extensions to the brand if I think the domain is worth keeping and flipping.
Don't tell me there are no investors in the country you are from that are willing to buy your domain or your brand.

The best way to secure your brand is to trademark it and patent the products.

New Business Startup Company.

Imagine how much money you could save by having a keyword related domain?

Yes brandable names are fine providing your product or service is well known, but what if you are starting out and want the world to know who you are?

This is where SEO link wheels come in. So you have launched your brandable website which is not known to the world and probably people will not even search for your name so what do you do?

You then hire a marketing company to advertise your name. Imagine if there was a simpler way to get on the first page of google with a keyword related domain.

What you do is you launch your site which is the mothership but you also launch another forwarded to you main site with your keyword related domain. This is called a 'SEO Link Wheel' The name will change in your address bar on your browser automatically showing you your branded site. **By merely forwarding a keyword domain name to your default site other than the name change it does nothing for your business but if you develop an independant website, landing page or blog you are theorectically creating a backlink to your main website.**

CHAPTER THIRTY

The Money Laundering, Terrorist Financing and Transfer of Funds (Information on the Payer) Regulations 2017

http://www.legislation.gov.uk/uksi/2017/692/made

A law in the UK requires Businesses that have high ticket sales to vett their clients. This applies to sellers and buyers of high value digital assets.
Customer due diligence requirements:

What customer due diligence is.

Customer due diligence means taking steps to identify your customers and checking they are who they say they are. In practice this means obtaining a customer's:

1) name

2) photograph on an official document which confirms their identity

3) residential address and date of birth
The best way to do this is to ask for a government issued document like a passport, along with utility bills, bank statements and other official documents.

Other sources of customer information include the electoral register and information held by credit reference agencies such as Experian and Equifax.You also need to identify the 'beneficial owner' in certain situations.

This may be because someone else is acting on behalf of another person in a particular transaction, or it may be because you need to establish the ownership structure of a company, partnership or trust.

As a general rule, the beneficial owner is the person who's behind the customer and who owns or controls the customer. Or it's the person on whose behalf a transaction or activity is carried out.

If you have doubts about a customer's identity, you mustn't continue to deal with them until you're sure.

When you need to apply customer due diligence measures

You must apply customer due diligence measures:

When you establish a business relationship with a customer (or another party in a property sale when you suspect money laundering or terrorist financing when you have doubts about a customer's identification information that you obtained previously when it's necessary for existing customers - for example if their circumstances change if you aren't a high value dealer, when you carry out an **'occasional transaction' worth €15,000 or moreas a high value dealer, when you: make a payment to a supplier worth €10,000 or more carry out an 'occasional transaction' worth €10,000 or more**.

CHAPTER THIRTY ONE

Conclusion

My Final Recommendations.

Here is a quideline of things you can do to get your domains sold other than stating the obvious of listing on Godaddy, Flippa, Sedo Afternic to name a few and ourselves :-) etc.

1) Create a Landing Page and do some Seo. If you don't upload your domain to all the search engines, how do you expect them to list you, never mind find you?

2) Create a blog, be consistent and write something a couple times a week.

3) As above list to reputable Domain Broker sites.

4) Advertise on all the social media platforms.

5) Find Groups and Pages on Social Media that you can join.

6) Search Google for similar names as your Domain and especially concentrate on the ones that are not on the first page of Google for example.

The companies will appreciate the value of your domain if the keywords match your domain name to help them rank better. However before you contact anyone do make sure your domain has value, no one wants to be bothered in their busy schedule with inferior domain names.

7) Remember to use charm pricing. Rather than list something for £2000, list it instead for £1,999.99 its only one penny less but it looks less and more pleasing to the eye.

8) Search for hashtags that end with your domain name and contact the people behind them.

9) Paid Per Click Advertising tells you the end user needs help being on the first page of Google. Do not approach a company that has a natural listing as they will not see the value of what you are trying to sell them.

10) Try Angel Investors. There are plenty of companies advertising investors waiting for an opportunity to knock.

11) Consider approaching investment companies.

12) Make classified ads - read their t&c first not all companies allow digital products.

13) Consider putting an advert in a local newspaper under the business section.

14) Attend trade shows compatible with your niche.

15) Research local businesses that need help with marketing and appoach them with your business plan. Also do your due diligence and evalutate your domains do not use the online bots like www.estibot.com they are not accurate.

I recommend either using Google Keyword Planner which you can find when you set up Google Adwords or www.serps.com they have 30 days free trial. Google on the other hand is free to use, but you need to set up a Gmail account with them before using this service.

I hope you enjoyed reading this book just as much as I had writing it. It serves as a reference for budding Domainers from newbie's to the more experienced. It also teaches business's the value of domain names and that domain names should not be taken for granted, as once they have gone they are usually gone forever. So if you see a domain available do not wait as the next time you check the availability if it is a good keyword the chances are it would most probably have gone.

During my journey of learning I have been able to accumulate a lot of knowledge in starting business's from scratch. I help companies succeed and help them generate traffic. Regardless of your needs or your budget I am here on hand to help you prosper.

Feel free to contact me to answer any questions you may have.

Renata Barnes
info@startbrand.co.uk

SERVICES

Domain Brokering, Website Design, SEO, SMO, Business Consultancy, Advertising, Ecommerce, Online & Offline Distribution, Marketing, Internet Marketing, Social Media Marketing, Technology, App Design, Affiliate Marketing, Corporate Stationary Design and Branding, Re-Branding, Books/eBooks Design, Blog Posts, Rewriting, Custom Writing, Articles, Copywriting, Press Release, Proofreading, Ghostwriting, Content Writing, Freelance Writing, Photo Restoration, Corporate & Commercial Photography.

YOUR NOTES

YOUR NOTES

YOUR NOTES

Lightning Source UK Ltd.
Milton Keynes UK
UKRC022135011118
331618UK00001B/28